A Readers Theatre Treasury of Stories

Win Braun and Carl Braun

Illustrated by Win Braun

PORTAGE &
MAIN PRESS

Layout design by Henry John Epp

Printed in Canada

Portage & Main Press
100 - 318 McDermot Ave.
Winnipeg, Manitoba, Canada
R3A 0A2

E-mail: books@portageandmainpress.com
Fax: 1-866-734-8477
Tel: 204-987-3500
Toll Free: 1-800-667-9673

CONTENTS

READERS THEATRE
AT HOME AND SCHOOL

What is Readers Theatre?

Readers Theatre is a cooperative or shared reading of a poem, story or lyrics of a favourite song. Two or more readers can take part. Even if a piece is scripted for only two readers, and you want more than two readers to participate, assign parts to a duet or chorus. And there are times when you will want to give a part to a weaker and stronger reader for practice, so that one reader supports the other till both feel comfortable enough to read independently. Simple as that. And children love to read cooperatively with older brothers and sisters, parents and teachers, even grandparents.

Readers Theatre requires no memorizing, and no costumes, although at times children may demand costumes. That's fine! Even then, discarded cool shades, hats, shoes, shawls and sashes from the "dress-up" box are more than sufficient. It is important, though, that Readers Theatre be kept simple enough so that you will want to do it often — at bedtime, after school, at any time during the day.

Why Readers Theatre?

It's fun! Even for turned-off readers, it is a **turn-on**. It's fun for the most fluent reader who wants **new challenges**, new channels for her creative energies. It has the potential to generate more enthusiasm and more excitement than most reading activities. What's more, it's fun for parents and teachers.

Readers Theatre is a **supportive** activity. The reader is safe to experiment and take **risks** as **cooperation** rather than competition is valued. If a piece is too difficult the first time around, we simply read along with the reader or allow him to follow a taped reading till he is able to read independently.

Readers Theatre provides more meaningful engagement for all readers than any other reading activity. Whereas weaker readers often become overwhelmed, frequently passive, in more traditional environments, they become **actively involved** in Readers Theatre, often surprising themselves as much as others how well they are able to perform. And built-in **success** is the hallmark of Readers Theatre. Just ask children, teachers and parents who have tried it. As one teacher put it recently, "By mistake I allowed Terry to select a part that I knew was far too difficult for him. I was really worried. I didn't want to discourage him by assigning an easier part, but I also didn't want him to experience failure and discouragement. Well, he came back the next morning with the most enthusiastic, 'I can read my part real good.' And that was an understatement. He must have worked all night at the piece. He just shocked us all by his superb rendition. I was so wrong, so very wrong. I wonder how often I underestimate the abilities of children."

Readers Theatre is one of the best means for children to **learn to hear themselves**, listen to themselves as they try to improve their reading to emulate the best reading they have heard from their parents, teachers or more competent friends. Learning to listen to oneself is one of surest ways for children to improve not only their reading, but also their writing. And yes, spelling improves markedly with improved ability to listen to oneself.

Involvement in Readers Theatre is a guarantee for improved **fluent reading**. This is true especially with the use of verse and song. The **rhyme and rhythm** of language enables readers to use larger and larger chunks of print, going beyond the word by word reading that is typical of the weaker reader. And the increasing ability to read with more ease and fluency is one of best guarantees that children will want to spend more time reading.

Readers Theatre invites **celebration** and **performance.** Even the most withdrawn child is moved to **practice**, to listen to herself to see what needs to be improved, and then **practice** some more once she has felt the warmth, support and encouragement that comes from a captive audience. That is likely the **magic** behind Readers Theatre. And the audience may consist of a grandparent, a principal, friends, and for special celebration, the PTA or the school assembly. Even the goal of preparing a piece for taping is enough for many children to keep working on a piece. You will be amazed at the sudden boost to the young reader's **confidence.**

Readers Theatre is for everyone. There isn't a reader anywhere who is unable to participate. The child who is just beginning to follow print, the ESL child, the so-called disabled reader, anyone can work together to produce a Readers Theatre. And that is another benefit. No segregation, no grouping of buzzards and bluebirds. They can all become bluebirds — if we believe in our abilities as parents and teachers, and if we **believe in the creative abilities of our children.**

SUGGESTIONS FOR USE OF THIS BOOK

Once you start working with Readers Theatre, you really won't need anyone to suggest what to do. You will come up with many ways of adding interest and variation to the readings. We simply offer a few suggestions to help you get started.

1. Aim to make all reading free of stress. If a child is reluctant or fearful, read his part with him giving only as much support as necessary. Some groups will benefit from reading the entire piece in chorus as a "warm up," and then move into reading in parts.

2. Some children, especially those children who have already experienced difficulty in reading, will do well to have a taped version of the entire piece as a resource. A child may read along through an entire piece, or simply check to see how her own part is read. For many this is a kind of security blanket till they become comfortable with Readers Theatre and till they discover that they are capable of more than they thought.

3. As an "at home" activity, many of the pieces will suggest more parts than the number of children available. No problem! One person can take a chorus part; one person (often an adult) can be assigned to read the parts of two readers. Or larger chunks of the piece can be read by two or three people in the form of chorus reading.

4. Encourage children to be on the lookout for poetry or song lyrics that they can script for Readers Theatre. Scripting a piece makes a wonderful group or individual writing activity. And what a boost to children's ability to listen to their own reading as they refine their scripts. And improved listening, again, is going to mean a boost to their writing.

5. Encourage children to experiment with their voices as they read. Record their renditions and encourage them to talk about what they like about their reading, and what they want to change in future readings.

6. Make Readers Theatre a significant part of your home and school reading program. Give it high profile, including children's own scripts and tapes of their renditions (including pieces done at home) as part of their portfolios. You will find that even some of the more dramatic nursery rhymes, the Shel Silverstein or Denis Lee poetry, or "The Night Before Christmas," take on new life.

7. In order to involve the whole class, display a script on overhead transparencies, especially for some of the shorter pieces. Assign groups of children to read specific parts. This is a way of providing a safe environment for children to become comfortable with the various reader parts in a script. It also allows children the security to experiment with ideas for using voice effectively to portray character. The fairy tales and fables are especially appropriate for whole class (or larger group) reading.

8. We highly recommend that you encourage children to read some of the original, colour-illustrated versions of some of the pieces included in this book. A number of the selections appear in beautifully-illustrated form in an anthology (Strategies) series published by Nelson Canada in 1989, and by American Guidance Services in 1990. Check out the wonderfully-illustrated *A Lion in the Night* by Pamela Allen, *The Crocodile's Toothbrush* by Boris Zakhoder, Esphyr Slobodkina's *Caps for Sale,* or one of many illustrated versions of *The Night Before Christmas*. Children are encouraged when they discover that they are able to read independently what they have read as a Reader's Theatre earlier. And it's a tremendous boost to their confidence as they find new pleasure in the fluency that is emerging as a result.

9. Keep enjoyment at the forefront.

ACKNOWLEDGEMENTS

Our interest in Readers Theatre has evolved over many years as we have observed children in classrooms and children in less formal settings become involved in chanting rhymes and rhythms, sometimes alone, but more often with other children or adults. It has been especially thrilling to see children become "hooked" for the first time as they become involved in a non-threatening, supportive Readers Theatre activity. We have seen this with children who are fluent readers, children who are anything but fluent, floundering, turned-off readers, ESL children, emergent readers, older readers. These children have given us the encouragement needed to embark on this venture, and we thank them for showing us what should have been obvious. We thank the many teachers and parents who have endorsed Readers Theatre as something that has "a special magic," something that has the potential to give all children their right to successful and enjoyable learning.

Grateful acknowledgement is also made for permission to reprint and script the following copyright material: *A Lion in the Night,* by Pamela Allen, copyright, 1985, Penguin Books Canada, permission by Curtis Brown (Aust) Pty Ltd Sydney; "Where's Willie?" copyright by author, Eve Bunting, permission of the author; "The Snake on Second Avenue," copyright, Adele Dueck, permission of the author; "Wait Till Martin Comes," by Maria Leach, reprinted by permission of Philomel Books from *The Thing at the Foot of the Bed and Other Scary Stories,* copyright, 1959, renewed, 1987, by MacDonald A. Leach; "Robot Doc," by Hazel Silliker, copyright (1988), permission by Paula Goepfert; "A Good Walk for Wags," copyright, 1995, by author, Amy Siamon-Rolf von den Baumen, permission by author; "The Snooks Family," from *Tales of Ebony* by Harcourt Williams, permission by Random House UK Limited; *The Crocodile's Toothbrush,* copyright, 1973, permission by McGraw-Hill, Inc.

A Lion in the Night

by Pamela Allen
for 4 readers & voices

by Pamela Allen

Reader 1: There once was a baby who lived in a castle with the King, the Queen, the Admiral, the Captain, the General, the Sergeant, and the little dog.

Reader 2: Because she was the baby she couldn't walk, and she couldn't talk.

Reader 3: But she could cry.

Reader 4: One night, when she had been put to bed while it was still light, she made a wish.

Reader 1: Later, when the moon was out and the tide was high, the Queen woke up.

Reader 2: And what did she see?

Voices: **She saw a lion stealing the baby.**

Reader 3: The Queen woke the King,

Reader 4: and the King woke the Admiral,

Reader 1: and the Admiral woke the Captain,

Reader 2: and the Captain woke the General,

Reader 3: and the General woke the Sergeant,

Reader 4: and the Sergeant woke the little dog, and

Voices: **What did they do?**

Reader 1: They *chased* the lion.

Reader 2: The lion that was stealing the baby.

Reader 3: Out of the castle and over the fields.

Reader 4: Over the fields and into the forest.

Reader 1: Out of the forest and past the church.

Reader 2: Past the church and into the boat.

Reader 3: Into the boat and across the sea.

Reader 4: Across the sea and over the mountains.

Reader 1: Over the mountains and into the fields.

Voices: **And there the lion stopped. Grrrrrrrrrr . . . . RRRAAH**

Reader 2: Back home they ran as fast as they could.

Reader 1: Over the mountains

Reader 2: into the boat

Reader 3: across the sea

Reader 4: past the church

Reader 1: into the forest

Reader 2: and through the fields

Voices: **but . . . GGRRRRR**

Lion: **Ha! Ha!** *I'm the King of the castle and you're the dirty rascals,*

Reader 3: bellowed the lion.

Reader 4: He'd got there first and fooled them all.

Reader 1: Now the game was over, everyone except the lion and the baby was very tired.

Reader 2: And everyone as well as the lion and the baby was very hungry.

Reader 3: So the lion invited them all in for breakfast.

Reader 4: They had what they usually had for breakfast;

Reader 1: all except the lion, who gave the baby her bottle,

Reader 2:   tied a napkin around his neck,

Reader 3:   then gobbled up . . .

Reader 4:   . . . one bowl of porridge,

Reader 1:   two eggs,

Reader 2:   a slice of hot buttered toast,

Reader 3:   some crumpets,

Reader 4:   bread and honey,

Reader 1:   fruit yoghurt,

Reader 2:   muesli,

Reader 3:   a bag of biscuits belonging to the little dog,

Reader 4:   and last of all,

Reader 1:   a big bowl of strawberries and red jelly.

Reader 2:   Then, because it was morning

Reader 3:   the lion . . .

Voices: **just disappeared.**

Go to the library and find the original version of the beautifully illustrated *A Lion in the Night* by Pamela Allen, Penguin Books (Puffin Paperback) in Canada, 1985. Read it all by yourself. You will find other books by the same author like *Bertie and the Bear, Mr. Archimedes' Bath, Who Sank the Boat?* Each book has special surprises for the reader.

A Readers Theatre Treasury of Stories   *Braun & Braun*

retold by Win Braun
for 8 readers

Henny Penny

retold by Win Braun

Reader 1:	Early one morning, Henny Penny was looking for some food.
Henny Penny:	**Peck, peck, peck.**
Reader 2:	went Henny Penny as she pecked under the old oak tree for seeds and juicy bugs.
Reader 1:	Suddenly, an acorn fell from the tree and hit Henny Penny on her head.
Reader 2:	Surprised, she ran around and yelled,
Henny Penny:	**Cluck! Cluck!** *The sky is falling! The sky is falling!* I must go and tell the King!
Reader 1:	Along the way Henny Penny met Cocky Locky.
Cocky Locky:	*Cock-a-doodle-doo!* Where are you going in such a hurry?
Henny Penny:	**Cluck! Cluck!** *The sky is falling! The sky is falling!* I must go and tell the King!
Cocky Locky:	May I go with you?
Reader 2:	asked Cocky Locky.
Henny Penny:	Yes, but we must hurry.
Reader 1:	And off Henny Penny and Cocky Locky went to tell the King.

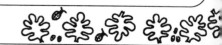

Reader 2:	Soon they met Goosey Loosey.
Goosey Loosey:	**Honk! Honk!** Where are you going in such a hurry?
HP and CL:	*The sky is falling! The sky is falling!*
	We must go and tell the King!
Reader 1:	said Henny Penny and Cocky Locky.
Goosey Loosey:	May I go with you?
Reader 2:	asked Goosey Loosey.
HP and CL:	Yes, but we must hurry.
Reader 1:	And off Henny Penny, Cocky Locky and Goosey Loosey went to tell the King.
Reader 2:	Soon they met Ducky Lucky.
Ducky Lucky:	**Quack! Quack!** Where are you going in such a hurry?
HP, CL, and GL:	*The sky is falling! The sky is falling!*
	We must go and tell the King!
Ducky Lucky:	May I go with you?
Reader 1:	asked Ducky Lucky.
HP, CL, and GL:	Yes, but we must hurry.
Reader 2:	And off Henny Penny, Cocky Locky, Goosey Loosey and Ducky Lucky went to tell the King.
Reader 1:	Soon they met Turkey Lurkey.
Turkey Lurkey:	**Gobble! Gobble! Gobble!** Where are you going in such a hurry?
HP, CL, GL and DL:	*The sky is falling! The sky is falling!*
	We must go and tell the King!
Turkey Lurkey:	May I go with you?
Reader 2:	asked Turkey Lurkey.

HP, CL, GL and DL: Yes, but we must hurry.

Reader 1:   And off Henny Penny, Cocky Locky, Goosey Loosey, Ducky Lucky and Turkey Lurkey went to tell the King.

Reader 2:   It was not long before they met Foxy Loxy, a very sly fox.

Foxy Loxy: Where are you going in such a hurry?

Reader 1:   asked Foxy Loxy.

HP, CL, GL, DL and TL: *The sky is falling! The sky is falling!* We must go and tell the King!

Foxy Loxy: I know the way to the King's castle. Come with me.

Reader 2:   said Foxy Loxy.

HP, CL, GL, DL and TL: Thank you. Thank you.

Reader 1:   said Henny Penny, Cocky Locky, Goosey Loosey, Ducky Lucky and Turkey Lurkey.

Reader 2:   They followed Foxy Loxy to his cave.

Reader 1:   They went right in, and Foxy Loxy locked the door.

Reader 2:   No one ever saw Henny Penny, Cocky Locky, Goosey Loosey, Ducky Lucky and Turkey Lurkey again.

Reader 1:   And the King was never told that the sky was falling down.

Reader 2:   Foxy Loxy looked a little fatter at the end of that day

Reader 1:   and he settled down for a long nap.

A Readers Theatre Treasury of Stories  Braun & Braun

The Three Bears

retold by Win Braun
for 8 readers

retold by Win Braun

Reader 1: Once upon a time there were three bears.

Reader 2: They lived in a little house deep in the forest.

Reader 3: Early one morning, Mama Bear made porridge for breakfast.

Reader 4: It was very hot, so the three bears decided to take a walk in the forest while the porridge cooled.

Reader 1: Soon, a little girl named Goldilocks wandered into the forest, deep and dark, and found the bears' little house.

Reader 2: Goldilocks knocked on the door.

All: ***Knock, knock, knock.***

Reader 3: No one answered, so she opened the door and walked right in.

All: Creak, creak, creak.
Stomp, stomp, stomp.

Reader 4: Goldilocks saw the three bowls of porridge on the table —

All: A great, big bowl,
A middle-sized bowl,
And a wee, little bowl.

Reader 1: She was very hungry, so she tasted the great, big bowl of porridge.

All: It was ***too*** hot!

Reader 2: Next she tasted the middle sized bowl of porridge.

All: It was ***too*** cold!

A Readers Theatre Treasury of Stories *Braun & Braun*

Reader 3: Finally she tasted the wee, little bowl of porridge.

All: And it was *just* right!

Readers 1 and 2: So she finished every drop.

All: *Slurp! Slurp! Slurp!*

Reader 4: Goldilocks felt a little tired, so she went into the living room.

Reader 1: There she found three chairs —

All: A great, big chair,
A middle-sized chair,
And a wee, little chair.

Reader 2: Goldilocks sat in the great, big chair.

All: It was *too* high!

Reader 3: Then she sat in the middle-sized chair.

All: It was *too* wide!

Reader 4: Finally she sat in the wee, little chair.

All: It was *just* right!

Reader 1: But Goldilocks was too big, and the chair broke into pieces.

All: *Crack!* Crunch! Crash!

Reader 2: Goldilocks yawned. She was very sleepy, so she went upstairs.

Reader 3: There she found three beds —

All: A great big bed,

A middle-sized bed,

And a wee, little bed.

Reader 4: She got into the **great, big bed.**

All: It was *too* hard!

Reader 1: Then she got into the middle-sized bed.

All: It was *too* soft!

Reader 2: Finally she snuggled under the covers on the wee, little bed.

All: It was *just* right!

Reader 3: Soon she was fast asleep.

Reader 4: Meanwhile, the three bears had arrived home.

Reader 1: They were very hungry and ready for breakfast.

Readers 2 and 3: But what did they find?

Readers 1 and 4: Someone had been in their house!

Papa Bear: **Someone has been tasting my porridge,**

Reader 2: said Papa Bear in his **great, booming voice.**

Mama Bear: Someone has been tasting my porridge,

Reader 3: said Mama Bear in her middle-sized voice.

Baby Bear: And someone has been tasting *my* porridge,

Reader 4: said Baby Bear in his wee, little voice,

Baby Bear: and ate it *all* up!

Reader 1: They went over to their chairs.

Papa Bear: **Someone has been sitting in my chair,**

Reader 2: said Papa Bear in his **great, booming voice.**

Mama Bear: Someone has been sitting in my chair,

Reader 3: said Mama Bear in her middle-sized voice.

Baby Bear: Someone has been sitting in *my* chair,

Reader 4: said Baby Bear in his wee, little voice,

A Readers Theatre Treasury of Stories Braun & Braun©

Baby Bear:	and has broken it to pieces!
Reader 1:	By this time, the three bears were very upset.
Reader 2:	They stomped upstairs.
All:	**Stomp! Stomp! Stomp!**
Papa Bear:	**Someone has been lying on my bed,**
Reader 3:	said Papa Bear in his great, booming voice.
Mama Bear:	Someone has been lying on my bed,
Reader 4:	said Mama Bear in her middle-sized voice.
Baby Bear:	Someone has been lying on *my* bed,
Reader 1:	said Baby Bear in his wee, little voice,
Baby Bear:	and here she is!
Goldilocks:	*Aaaaaah!*
Reader 2:	screamed Goldilocks when she saw the three bears glaring at her.
Reader 3:	She jumped out of bed
All:	**Thump!**
Reader 4:	and ran down the stairs and out of the house.
Reader 1:	Goldilocks ran straight home,
Readers 2 and 3:	*and never,*
Readers 1 and 4:	*never*
Reader 2:	went into the forest again.

Caps for Sale

by Esphyr Slobodkina
for 6 readers & monkeys

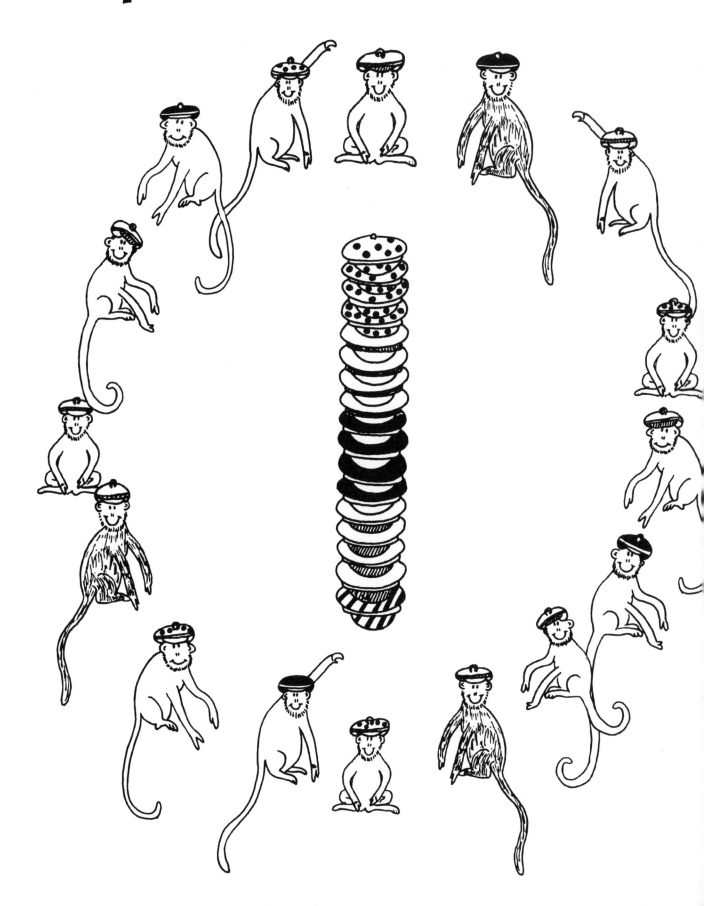

by Esphyr Slobodkina

Reader 1: Once there was a peddler who went out to sell caps. He carried the caps on top of his head.

Reader 2: First he put on his own striped cap,

Reader 3: then four yellow caps,

Reader 4: then four blue caps,

Reader 5: then the four red caps,

All: and on the very top four polkadot caps.

Reader 1: He walked up and down the streets, holding himself very straight,

Reader 2: so as not to upset his caps.

Reader 3: As he went along he called,

Peddler: *Caps! Caps for sale! Fifty cents a cap!*

Reader 4: But nobody bought any caps that morning.

Reader 5: Not even a red cap.

Reader 1: In time the peddler began to feel very hungry,

Reader 2: but he had no money for lunch.

Reader 3: Not even a taco.

Reader 4: So he walked and walked until he came to a great big tree.

Peddler: This is a nice place to rest,

Reader 5: thought he.

Reader 1: So he sat down, under the tree and leaned back little by little against the tree-trunk so as not to upset the caps on his head.

Reader 2: Then he reached up to make sure that they were straight —

Reader 3: first his own striped cap,

Reader 4: then the four yellow caps,

Reader 5: then the four blue caps,

Reader 1: then the four red caps,

Reader 2: then on the very top the four polkadot caps.

All: Then he went to sleep.

Reader 3: He slept for a long time.

Reader 4: When he woke up, he reached up to make sure that his caps were still on his head.

Reader 5: All he felt was his own striped cap!

All: *The other caps were gone.*

Reader 1: He looked to the right of him.

All: *No caps.*

Reader 2: He looked to the left of him.

All: *No caps.*

Reader 3: He looked behind the tree.

All: *No caps.*

Reader 4: Then — he looked up into the tree.

Reader 5: And what do you think he saw?

Reader 1: On every branch there was a monkey.

Reader 2: On every monkey there was a cap —

Reader 3: a yellow cap,

Reader 4: or a blue cap,

Reader 5: or a red cap,

Reader 1: or a polkadot cap.

Reader 2: The peddler looked at the monkeys.

Reader 3: The monkeys looked at the peddler.

Reader 4: He shook a finger at the monkeys and said,

Peddler: *You monkeys, you! Give me back my caps!*

Reader 5: The monkeys only shook their fingers back at him and said,

Monkeys: Tsz, tsz, tsz.

Reader 1: This made the peddler angry, so he shook his fist at the monkeys and said,

Peddler: *You monkeys, you! Give me back my caps!*

Reader 2: But the monkeys only shook their fists back at him and said,

Monkeys: Tsz, tsz, tsz.

Reader 3: Now the peddler was quite angry.

Reader 4:   He stamped his foot, and said,

Peddler: *You monkeys, you! Give me back my caps!*

Reader 5:   But the monkeys only stamped their feet back at him and said,

Monkeys: Tsz, tsz, tsz.

Reader 1:   At last the peddler became so angry that he pulled off his cap and threw it on the ground.

Reader 2:   Then, each monkey pulled off his cap...

Reader 3:   and all the yellow caps...

Reader 4:   and all the blue caps...

Reader 5:   and all the red caps...

All: and all the polkadot caps. . . *came flying down out of the tree.*

Reader 1:   So the peddler picked up his caps and put them back on his head —

Reader 2:   first his own striped cap,

Reader 3:   then the four yellow caps,

Reader 4:   then the four blue caps,

Reader 5:   then the four red caps,

Reader 1:   then the four polkadot caps on the very top.

All: And slowly, he walked away calling,

Peddler: *Caps! Caps for sale! Fifty cents a cap!*

A Readers Theatre Treasury of Stories   Braun & Braun©

The

Teeny Tiny

Woman

An Old English Ghost Tale
retold by Win Braun
for 4 readers & voice

THE TEENY TINY WOMAN

An Old English Ghost Tale
retold by Win Braun

Reader 1: Once, long ago, there lived a teeny tiny woman who lived in a teeny tiny cottage.

Reader 2: One morning the teeny tiny woman put on her teeny tiny coat and her teeny tiny hat

Reader 3: and went out for a teeny tiny walk.

Reader 1: When she had walked a teeny tiny way, she came to a teeny tiny fence.

Reader 2: The teeny tiny woman opened a teeny tiny gate in the teeny tiny fence

Reader 3: and in a teeny tiny moment she was in a teeny tiny churchyard.

Reader 1: In the teeny tiny churchyard the teeny tiny woman found a teeny tiny bone.

Reader 2: She found the teeny tiny bone on a teeny tiny grave.

Teeny Tiny Woman: This teeny tiny bone will make a fine teeny tiny soup for my teeny tiny dinner.

Reader 3: said the teeny tiny woman.

Reader 1: So she put the teeny tiny bone into her teeny tiny bag and took it home to her teeny tiny cottage.

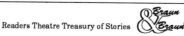A Readers Theatre Treasury of Stories

Reader 2: The teeny tiny woman was a teeny tiny bit tired after her teeny tiny walk.

Reader 3: So she went up the teeny tiny stairs, put the teeny tiny bone into her teeny tiny wardrobe, and crawled under the teeny tiny blanket on her teeny tiny bed.

Reader 1: The teeny tiny woman was fast asleep in a teeny tiny while.

Reader 2: But a teeny tiny time later she was awakened by a teeny tiny voice from the teeny tiny wardrobe which said,

Voice: Give me my bone!

Reader 1: This frightened the teeny tiny woman a teeny tiny bit, so she pulled her teeny tiny blanket up over her teeny tiny head a teeny tiny bit and soon was asleep again.

Reader 2: She was awakened a teeny tiny time later by the teeny tiny voice which called once again from the teeny tiny wardrobe, this time, a teeny tiny bit louder,

Voice: Give me my bone!

Reader 3: This frightened the teeny tiny woman a teeny tiny bit more, so she pulled her teeny tiny blanket up over her teeny tiny head a teeny tiny bit further.

Reader 1:   Once again, she was awakened after a teeny tiny time by the teeny tiny voice from the teeny tiny wardrobe which called out a teeny tiny bit louder,

Voice: # Give me my bone!

Reader 2:   This frightened the teeny tiny woman a teeny tiny bit more,

Reader 3:   but she pulled down her teeny tiny blanket and said in her loudest and bravest teeny tiny voice,

Teeny Tiny Woman: # Take it!

by Clement Moore
for 6 readers

The Night Before Christmas

THE NIGHT BEFORE CHRISTMAS

by Clement Moore

Reader 1: 'Twas the night before Christmas when all through the house

Reader 2: Not a creature was stirring,

Reader 3: Not even a mouse.

Reader 4: The stockings were hung by the chimney with care

Reader 5: In hopes that Saint Nicholas soon would be there.

Reader 1: The children were nestled all snug in their beds,

Reader 2: While visions of sugarplums danced in their heads.

Reader 3: And Mamma in her kerchief and I in my cap,

Reader 4: Had just settled our brains for a long winter's nap;

Reader 5: When out on the lawn there arose such a clatter,

Reader 1: I sprang from my bed to see what was the matter.

Reader 2: Away to the window I flew like a flash,

Reader 3: Tore open the shutters and threw up the sash.

Reader 4: The moon on the breast of the new-fallen snow

Reader 5: Gave a luster of midday to objects below,

Reader 1: When, what to my wondering eyes should appear,
But a miniature sleigh and eight tiny reindeer,

Reader 2: With a little old driver so lively and quick,
I knew in a moment it must be Saint Nick.

Reader 3: More rapid than eagles his coursers they came,

Reader 4: And he whistled and shouted and called them by name:

Santa: *Now, Dasher! Now, Dancer! Now, Prancer and Vixen!*
On, Comet! On, Cupid! On, Donner and Blitzen!

Reader 5:   To the top of the porch,

Reader 1:   To the top of the wall!

Reader 2:   Now, dash away!

Reader 3:   Dash away!

Reader 4:   Dash away all!

Reader 5:   As dry leaves that before the wild hurricane fly,
When they meet with an obstacle mount to the sky,

Reader 1:   So up to the housetop the coursers they flew
With a sleigh full of toys,

Reader 2:   and Saint Nicholas too.

Reader 3:   And then in a twinkling I heard on the roof
The prancing and pawing of each little hoof.

Reader 4:   As I drew in my head and was turning around,
Down the chimney Saint Nicholas came with a bound.

Reader 5:   He was dressed all in fur from his head to his foot,

Reader 1:   And his clothes were all tarnished with ashes and soot.

Reader 2:   A bundle of toys he had flung on his back,

Reader 3:   And he looked like a peddler just opening his pack.

Reader 4:   His eyes — how they twinkled!

Reader 5:   His dimples — how merry!

Reader 1:   His cheeks were like roses, his nose like a cherry.

Reader 2:   His droll little mouth was drawn up like a bow,

Reader 3: And the beard on his chin was as white as the snow.

Reader 4: The stump of his pipe he held tight in his teeth,

Reader 5: And the smoke it encircled his head like a wreath.

Reader 1: He had a broad face and a round little belly

Reader 2: That shook when he laughed like a bowl full of jelly.

Reader 3: He was chubby and plump, a right jolly old elf,

Reader 4: And I laughed when I saw him in spite of myself.

Reader 5: A wink of his eye and a twist of his head

Soon gave me to know I had nothing to dread.

Reader 1: He spoke not a word but went straight to his work,

Reader 2: And filled all the stockings; then turned with a jerk,

Reader 3: And laying his finger aside of his nose,

Reader 4: And giving a nod, up the chimney he rose.

Reader 5: He sprang to his sleigh, to his team gave a whistle,

Reader 1: And away they all flew like the down of a thistle.

Reader 2: But I heard him exclaim ere he drove out of sight —

Santa: *Happy Christmas to all,*
And to all a Good Night!

A Readers Theatre Treasury of Stories Braun & Braun©

retold by Carl Braun
for 9 readers

Belling the Cat

retold by Carl Braun

Reader 1:   In a place called Wellington there were many mice.

Reader 2:   There were many frightened mice.

Reader 1:   They were frightened because Belling, the cat, had been sneaking around and snatching mice.

Reader 2:   The mice were worried and didn't know what to do.

Reader 3:   One day, they decided to call a meeting to make plans for dealing with Belling.

Reader 4:   The Mouse Chairperson called the meeting to order.

Mouse Chairperson: We have gathered here to decide what to do with Belling, the cat.

Mouse 1:   You're right! Something must be done.

Mouse 2:   Right! We must do something.

Mouse 3:   Right! We must do something soon.

Mouse 4:   Right! We must do something right now!

Mouse Chairperson: What can we do?

Mouse 1:   We can get a dog to chase the cat.

Mouse 2:   Right! We can get a dog to chase the cat. Then the cat will be too busy running from the dog to catch us.

Mouse 3:   Right! We must get a dog soon.

Mouse 4:   Right! We must get a dog right now!

Mouse Chairperson: Order! Order. We must have order!

Mouse 1:	Getting a dog is not a good idea. The dog and the cat will become friends, and then we will have double trouble.
Mouse 2:	But we must keep the cat from snatching our brothers and sisters.
Mouse 3:	I know what to do! Let's build a cage to catch the cat.
Mouse 4:	Right! Let's build a cage to catch the cat.
Mouse 1:	Right! Let's build a cage soon.
Mouse 2:	Right! Let's build a cage right now!
Mouse 3:	But it will take weeks to build a cage, and we must stop the cat right now.
Mouse 4:	I have an idea.
Reader 1:	And all the mice stopped to listen to the new idea.
Mouse 2:	We can tie the cat's mouth so that it can't snatch us.
Mouse 3:	Right! Let's tie up the cat's mouth.
Mouse 4:	Right! Let's tie up the cat's mouth with a long rope.
Mouse 1:	Right! Let's wind the rope around and around the cat's mouth.
Mouse 2:	Right! Let's tie up the cat's mouth right now.
Mouse 3:	But if we tie up her mouth, the cat won't be able to eat, and she'll starve.
Mouse 4:	Right! And then we won't have a cat at all. And everyone knows that mice should have a cat.
Mouse 1:	Right! Mice should have a cat.
Mouse 2:	Right! What would we do without a cat?
Mouse 3:	Right! We would have nothing to complain about without a cat.
Mouse 4:	Right! We would be bored without a cat.

Mouse Chairperson: Order! Order! We must come to order!

Mouse 1: I have an answer to our problem.
Reader 2: And all the ears turned to listen to him.

Mouse 3: We'll tie a bell around the cat's neck, and then we'll hear him when he tries to sneak up on us.
Mouse 4: Right! Then we can run and hide.
Mouse 1: Right! A bell around the cat's neck is the answer to our problem.
Mouse 2: Right! Then we can hear the cat coming.
Mouse 3: Right! Then we can run and hide.
Mouse 4: Right! We must bell the cat right now.

Reader 1: And all the mice finally agreed that they had found the answer to their problem.
Reader 2: They had forgotten only one thing.

Mouse Chairperson: Who will bell the cat?

Reader 3: This time not one mouse spoke.
Reader 4: There was complete silence.

Mouse Chairperson: Well, we have a solution to our problem, but who will bell the cat?

Reader 1: And there was a resounding chorus,

All Mice: Not I! Not I! Not I! Not I!

Readers 1 and 2: No problem is solved till somebody does the job.

A Readers Theatre Treasury of Stories Braun &Braun©

The Lion and the Mouse

retold by Carl Braun
for 10 readers

THE LION AND THE MOUSE

retold by Carl Braun

Reader 1: A mouse and a grasshopper were walking through the jungle one day.

Reader 2: In their path they could see something that looked like a large, brown rock.

Reader 3: And it blocked their path.

Reader 4: The mouse said,

Mouse: I'll have to climb over the rock.

Reader 1: The grasshopper said,

Grasshopper: I'll hop over and meet you on the other side.

Reader 2: As the mouse stepped on the brown thing, it began to move.

Reader 3: She saw immediately that she was standing on a lion's nose.

Reader 4: That brown rock turned out to be a lion.

Reader 1: The lion roared,

Lion: How dare you walk on my nose?

Reader 2: And while he was growling these words, he grabbed the tiny mouse in his paws.

Lion: Grrr...rrrr... Don't you know that I'm the King of the Jungle?

Reader 3: The mouse, of course, was very frightened and was just barely able to squeak,

Mouse: Please, oh, pleeea...se! Let me go, and someday I will help you in some way.

Reader 4:	The lion let out a loud roar,
Lion:	**GRRR....RRR...** How could a tiny mouse help the King of the Jungle?

Reader 1:	All the mouse could do was whimper in the smallest squeaks,
Mouse:	I don't know. But someday you will be glad that you made a friend of a tiny, tiny mouse.
Reader 2:	Once more the lion roared,
Lion:	Oh, well. You're of no use to me now. You may go.
Reader 3:	So the lion opened his paw and released the mouse.
Reader 4:	The mouse looked around for the grasshopper, who was hiding behind a blade of grass.

Reader 1:	The grasshopper was shaking with fright.
Reader 2:	It said,
Grasshopper:	Let's just hurry out of here. I can't talk my way out of things the way you can.
Reader 3:	The mouse and the grasshopper scurried home as fast as they could go.
Reader 4:	A few days later they heard a parrot calling through the jungle,
Parrot:	HELP! HELP! SOMEONE PLEASE HELP! The lion is caught.

Reader 1:	The mouse was the first to reply,
Mouse:	Where? Where is the lion?

Parrot:	By the waterfall.
Reader 2:	And with those words the mouse scampered away to the waterfall.
Mouse:	I must help the poor lion.
Reader 3:	When the mouse approached the waterfall, it saw that the lion was caught in a hunter's net. Many other animals were there to see what was going to happen.
Reader 4:	The lion roared a very sad roar,
Lion:	**Help! Help!** Please, get me out of here!
Reader 1:	The giraffe said,
Giraffe:	I wish that I could help you.
Reader 2:	The monkey said,
Monkey:	I'm sorry, but I know nothing about untying knots.
Reader 3:	The tiny mouse began to chew through the ropes with her sharp teeth. It chewed and chewed while all the animals just looked on.
Reader 4:	And to everybody's surprise, the lion was soon free.
Reader 1:	The lion bared his huge teeth, but this time in a smile.
Lion:	**Thank you, thank you,** tiny mouse. You have saved my life. I didn't know that a tiny animal like you could save the King of the jungle.

Readers 1, 2, 3, and 4: **Little creatures can be great friends.**

A Readers Theatre Treasury of Stories Braun & Braun©

retold by Carl Braun
for 14 readers

The Miller, the Boy and the Donkey

THE MILLER, THE BOY AND THE DONKEY

retold by Carl Braun

Reader 1: One hot summer afternoon, a miller decided to take his donkey to market and sell him.

Reader 2: He called his son to come and help him catch the donkey in the meadow.

Reader 3: They took some carrots to make the job easier.

Reader 4: Sure enough, as the son held the carrots for the donkey to see, the donkey came trotting towards him.

Reader 1: So, the donkey followed the son all the way to the house nibbling at just enough carrots to keep him moving along.

Reader 2: The miller and his son brushed and combed the donkey's coat till it was shiny and clean.

Reader 3: They polished the donkey's hooves until they sparkled.

Reader 4: They combed the donkey's mane until it was silky.

Miller: What a clean donkey we have,

Reader 1: said the miller.

Miller: We'll carry him to market so that his feet won't get dirty.

Reader 2: They hadn't gone far when they met a farmer.

Reader 3: The farmer looked amused, and said as he laughed,

Farmer: How silly! How absurd! Imagine anyone carrying a donkey!

Reader 4:	And the farmer burst out laughing again.
Farmer:	The donkey should be carrying you. How absolutely silly!
Reader 1:	The miller did not like to be laughed at, and he made the donkey walk.
Reader 2:	Before long, the miller's son said,
Son:	My legs are tired. I feel very weary.
Reader 3:	So the miller lifted his son on to the donkey's back.
Reader 4:	They had gone only a short distance when they met three merchants on their way to the market.

Reader 1:	When the merchants saw the boy on the donkey's back, they were angry, and together they shouted,
Merchants:	What a lazy lad you are! Get down at once and let the old man ride.
Reader 2:	The miller asked his son to get off the donkey's back, and he got on himself.
Reader 3:	But it was very hot, and soon the son started complaining.
Son:	I am very hot and very tired. I can't walk much further.
Reader 4:	The miller didn't listen to the son's complaining.

Reader 1:	But three girls on their way to the market had heard the son.
Reader 2:	They jeered at the miller.
Girls:	Shame on you, old man! How can you ride on the donkey's back when your poor boy limps wearily behind?
Reader 3:	So the miller told his son to climb up behind him, and they both rode on the donkey's back.

Reader 4: They were going along without difficulty when they passed a cathedral.

Reader 1: A priest stood by the side of the road with his mouth open in amazement.

Priest: How dare you treat your animal in such cruel fashion? How can such a small animal carry such a heavy burden? Have you no pity at all?

Reader 2: Reluctantly, the miller and his son got off the donkey's back and plodded along in the hot sun.

Reader 3: The donkey trotted happily beside the two.

Reader 4: When they got to the market, the people gawked in amazement.

Reader 1: What a dippy old man,

Reader 2: some were saying.

Reader 3: Others said,

Reader 4: Imagine, walking beside the animal when they could be riding. Are they crazy?

Reader 1: The miller and his son were very tired and quickly sold the animal to a kind farmer.

Reader 2: The miller's head ached from all the advice he had received on their journey.

Reader 3: He said to his son,

Miller: From now on, I will make up my own mind.

Readers 1, 2, 3, and 4: Trying to please everyone will drive you crazy.

A Readers Theatre Treasury of Stories Braun & Braun

retold by *Carl Braun*
for 9 readers

The Fox and the Goat

THE FOX AND THE GOAT

retold by Carl Braun

Reader 1: One very hot summer, all the streams and ponds had dried up.

Reader 2: The animals were very, very thirsty.

Reader 3: One day a sly old fox discovered a well full of water.

Reader 1: Before long a big ant crawled out of the well.

Reader 2: The ant said to herself,

Ant: This water is so cool and tastes so good. I must tell all my friends about the well.

Reader 3: The fox overheard the ant and thought to himself,

Fox: If the water is that good, I must have a drink. I am very, very thirsty.

Reader 1: The fox drank and drank and drank some more.

Reader 2: He was so full of water that he lost his balance and

Reader 3: fell into the well.

Reader 1: A few minutes later a goat walked by. He said,

Goat: I wonder if there is any water in that well.

Reader 2: Just then a bluebird flew out of the well.

Reader 3: The bluebird overheard the goat and said,

Bluebird: Oh yes, there is cool water down there. I must tell my friends about it.

A Readers Theatre Treasury of Stories Braun & Braun©

Reader 1: The fox called from the well,

Fox: Yes, Mrs. Goat, there is cool, cool water down here. Jump in and join me. But there isn't enough for the friends of the ant and the bluebird. Jump in and get some water before it is gone.

Reader 2: The goat was quick to answer,

Goat: I'm coming! I'm coming!

Reader 3: And before you knew it, the goat was in the well.

Reader 1: The fox's trick had worked.

Reader 2: He had found a way to escape from the well.

Reader 3: While the goat was drinking he said,

Fox: I've had enough to drink now, Mrs. Goat. I'll climb on your back and leap out of the well. Then you can have the rest of the water to yourself.

Reader 1: And so he did.

Reader 2: Before long the goat had drunk enough water and wanted to get out of the well, too.

Reader 3: She saw a frog swimming in the well and asked him for help.

Goat: Help! Help! Please help me out of the well. Let me climb on your back and then you can leap out yourself.

Reader 1: The frog couldn't believe his ears. He replied,

Frog: You are very funny. How could you possibly ride on my back?

Reader 2: The fox heard the goat's pleas for help and ran to the well. He laughed and laughed.

Fox: What a foolish animal you are. You should have been thinking before you jumped. HA! HA! HA! You are stuck, Mrs. Goat.

Reader 3: A little mouse overheard the fox and came over to talk to him.

Mouse: Mr. Fox, you are being terribly unfair. You tricked Mrs. Goat into jumping into the well. You are the only one who can help her get out.

Reader 1: The fox decided to listen to the mouse.

Reader 2: He found a rope and threw it to the goat.

Reader 3: As he did so, he said,

Fox: You lucky, lucky goat. Hold on to the rope, and I will pull you out. But next time, plan a way to get out **before** you jump in.

Reader 1, 2 and 3: Look before you leap.

retold by Carl Braun
for 10 readers

The Goose that Laid the Golden Egg

THE GOOSE THAT LAID THE GOLDEN EGG

retold by Carl Braun

Reader 1: Long ago, in a faraway land, lived a poor farmer and his wife.

Reader 2: One year there was little rain and their crops didn't grow.

Reader 3: Their food supply was so low that they were unable to feed their animals.

Reader 4: The farmer and his wife were worried that their animals would starve.

Reader 1: One day the farmer said to his wife,

Farmer: Our animals are very hungry and we cannot afford to feed them. What can we do?

Reader 2: The farmer's wife said very sadly,

Wife: I'm afraid that we will have to sell our animals to people who are able to care for them.

Reader 3: The farmer said,

Farmer: But our animals are our friends. We will be very lonely without them.

Reader 4: But in his heart the farmer knew that his wife was right. The next morning he went into the barn to give the animals the sad news.

A Readers Theatre Treasury of Stories · Braun & Braun©

Farmer:	Good morning, my fine friends.
Reader 1:	The hen was first to reply.
Hen:	**Cluck! Cluck!** It would be a better morning if we had something to eat. Where is our breakfast?
Reader 2:	The cow was next.
Cow:	**Moo! Moo!** Where is my breakfast?
Reader 3:	It was the sheep's turn to speak.
Sheep:	Baa! Baa! We are very hungry. What is happening? You used to take good care of us.
Farmer:	Taking care? I am here to talk to you about that.
Reader 4:	The farmer saw a silly grin on the goose's face, and he asked,
Farmer:	Aren't you hungry? Why are you laughing at me?
Reader 1:	The goose immediately assured the farmer,
Goose:	I am not laughing at you.
Reader 2:	Just then the farmer noticed something shiny under the smiling goose.
Farmer:	What have we here? What kind of egg is this? Why, it's a golden egg! Wonderful! Wonderful! Wife! Wife! Come here quickly!
Reader 3:	And the wife ran to the barn as fast as her legs could carry her.
Wife:	What's wrong? What is it? Why, it's a golden egg!
Reader 4:	The farmer and his wife had never been so happy.

Reader 1:   While they were rejoicing, the goose spoke up,

Goose: It *is* a golden egg. You have taken such good care of your animals. This is a reward for your kindness.

Wife: But, but, but a golden egg. We do not deserve such a generous reward.

Reader 2:   The farmer interrupted his wife.

Farmer: Yes, we do. We will take the egg to town and sell it. Then our problems will be over. Our animals will never have to be hungry again.

Reader 3:   So the farmer and his wife went to town and sold the egg. Now they were able to take good care of their animals.

Reader 4:   The farmer said,

Farmer: I will give my animals the best care. They will eat the best food, and they will sleep on the finest straw.

Reader 1:   And the farmer kept his word for a while.

Reader 2:   The goose laid a golden egg everyday.

Reader 3:   It wasn't long before the farmer was rich, and he became greedy.

Reader 4:   Some days he was so busy counting his money that he forgot to feed his animals.

Reader 1:   Before long he thought,

Farmer: One golden egg a day isn't very much. I know what I will do. I will kill the goose and take all the eggs inside her.

A Readers Theatre Treasury of Stories

Reader 2:	And that is exactly what he did. He killed the goose.
Reader 3:	But, alas! There were no eggs inside the goose.
Reader 4:	The farmer ran to his wife and cried,
Farmer:	The goose is dead, and there were no eggs inside her. What are we going to do now?
Reader 1:	The wife was very upset.
Reader 2:	And angry. She shouted,
Wife:	You foolish man! There is nothing we can do. Now we have neither our friend, the goose, nor the golden eggs.
Reader 1, 2, 3 and 4:	**Those who take too much may lose everything.**

The Ant

retold by Carl Braun
for 8 readers

&

the

Grasshopper

THE ANT AND THE GRASSHOPPER

retold by Carl Braun

Reader 1: Once there was a happy-go-lucky grasshopper who did nothing but play all summer long.

Reader 2: She sang and she danced, she danced and she sang.

Reader 1: One day a bee came along and asked,

Bee: Don't you ever stop playing? Don't you ever work?

Reader 2: The grasshopper was quick to answer.

Grasshopper: Me work! Never ever! Playing is so much fun. Don't you ever get tired of WORK, WORK, WORK?

Reader 1: The bee replied,

Bee: Now and then I do get tired, but winter is coming and I have to get ready for winter.

Reader 2: The grasshopper didn't even stop to listen to the bee. She called to the bear,

Grasshopper: Bear, bear, come here. I want you to play with me.

Reader 1: The bear didn't even look up. He was too busy to play.

Reader 2: He kept working as he called to the grasshopper,

Bear: No, thank you. I have no time to play. I have to find a cave for the winter so that I will be safe and comfortable.

Reader 1:   The grasshopper saw a goose landing on the lake nearby, and called to her,

Grasshopper: Goose, goose, come and play with me. I know a dance that we can do together.

Reader 2:   The goose hardly took time to answer, but said very quickly,

Goose: Dance? Dance? I have no time to dance. I am just passing through on my way to the south. I have to get there before it gets too cold for me.

Reader 1:   By this time the grasshopper was getting just a little discouraged, but when she saw the mole, she thought,

Grasshopper: There's the mole. I bet he will sing with me.

Reader 2:   So Grasshopper called to the mole,

Grasshopper: Come here mole. I have made up a nice song about moles. I want to sing it with you.

Reader 1:   The mole was busy digging, but looked up just long enough to say,

Mole: Can't you see how busy I am? I would like to sing with you, but not now. I must finish digging my home before the ground gets cold and hard.

Reader 2:   Poor grasshopper shook her head and said,

Grasshopper: Work! Work! Work! All they do is **work, work, work**. Nobody has time to play!

Reader 1:   She was getting quite discouraged.

A Readers Theatre Treasury of Stories &Braun Braun©

Reader 2: The days were getting cooler, and the leaves began to fall from the trees. The grasshopper went to see the ant.

Reader 1: She said,

Grasshopper: What a beautiful, beautiful day this is! Come and play in the leaves with me.

Reader 2: The ant looked at the grasshopper in disbelief, and replied,

Ant: Play? Play? What do you mean? I can't play with you. I have to store food for the long, cold winter.

Reader 1: The poor grasshopper could not believe how anyone would want to work on such a beautiful day.

Reader 2: How could anyone think about winter on such a fine day!

Reader 1: The ant felt sorry for the grasshopper and said,

Ant: Winter will be here soon, and food will be hard to find. Come with me and I will help you find food.

Reader 2: The grasshopper was not interested in the least. She said,

Grasshopper: You go on with your work, work, work! I will sing and dance. You are missing all the fun.

Reader 1: Soon the fine days were gone, just as the ant had warned.

Reader 2:	Bitter, cold winds blew the fallen leaves across the fields.
Reader 1:	The grasshopper stopped singing.
Reader 2:	She was too cold to dance.
Reader 1:	With a grasshopper limp, she struggled to the ant's home, and begged,
Grasshopper:	Please, ant, give me something to eat. I am cold and hungry.
Reader 2:	The ant did feel sorry for the grasshopper, but could only say,
Ant:	Why should I help you? What did you do all summer while I was getting ready for the winter?
Reader 1:	The poor grasshopper hung her head and said,
Grasshopper:	I played. I danced. I sang.
Reader 2:	And the ant replied,
Ant:	Yes, while I worked you played and danced and sang. Go away now, and play and dance and sing.
Readers 1 and 2:	**Get ready today for what you will need tomorrow.**

A Readers Theatre Treasury of Stories

The Fox Without a Tail

retold by Carl Braun
for 10 readers

THE FOX WITHOUT A TAIL

retold by Carl Braun

Reader 1: There once was a very young fox who lived in a forest.

Reader 2: One day when he was out hunting, his tail got caught in a trap.

Reader 3: It didn't matter how hard he tried, his tail was stuck.

Reader 4: A beaver came by and saw that the fox was in trouble.

Reader 1: When the beaver saw that the fox's tail was caught, he said,

Beaver: I see that your tail is caught in a trap that was set for me. Let me help you.

Reader 2: So the fox and the beaver struggled to open the trap.

Reader 3: But, no matter how hard they tried, the trap would not open.

Reader 4: When the trap wouldn't open, the fox finally said,

Fox: Since we're not able to open the trap, I guess I'll have to leave my tail in the trap.

Beaver: Yes, that is what you will have to do.

Reader 1: The fox was able to pull himself from the trap.

Reader 2: But, without his beautiful tail.

Reader 3: He was very sad.

Reader 4: As he stealthily crept through the forest he kept to the shadows so that the other animals wouldn't see him.

A Readers Theatre Treasury of Stories

Reader 1:	An opossum hanging from a tree noticed the fox.
Reader 2:	And it noticed the missing tail.
Opossum:	Ha, ha, ha! How silly you look. A fox with nothing but a stub of a tail. Ha, ha, ha!
Reader 1:	The fox was sad enough and didn't need anyone to taunt him. He said,
Fox:	Don't laugh at me. Someday you could find yourself without a tail.
Reader 2:	Feeling sorry for himself, the fox moved on muttering to himself,
Fox:	I will find someone to help me. The turkey has so many feathers. Maybe he will give some to me. I will tie them to my stub, and then I will have a real tail once more.
Reader 3:	The fox found the turkey and told him about his idea.
Reader 4:	But the turkey taunted the fox, saying,
Turkey:	*Gobble! Gobble! Gobble!* What a silly idea! A fox with turkey feathers for a tail! Feathers belong to birds, not foxes.
Reader 1:	Disappointed and discouraged, the fox ran off to see his friend, the racoon.
Fox:	You have such a beautiful tail. Mine was like that once. What should I do to get a tail like yours?
Racoon:	I don't know. Just don't ask me to cut off my tail and give it to you.

Reader 2: That gave the fox an idea. He knew that he was the only fox in the forest without a tail.

Reader 3: He called all the foxes together.

Reader 4: Slyly, he stood with his back against a tree so the other foxes would not see his missing tail.

Reader 1: He addressed the foxes in the friendliest way possible.

Fox: My dear friends. It is time for a change. We have been carrying these long, heavy tails for too long. They slow us down when we run. They get in the way when we sit. We don't need our tails any longer. We must cut them off!

Reader 2: An old fox was the first to speak.

Old Fox: What? How did you come up with such a silly idea? Why are you standing against the tree? Surely you haven't lost your tail!

Reader 3: The fox was very sad now. He said,

Fox: Yes, you guessed right! I lost my tail in a beaver trap. I am so ashamed to be the only fox without a tail. I wanted all the foxes to look just like me.

Reader 4: Once again the old fox spoke for all.

Old Fox: It must be terrible to be without a tail. But surely you don't expect us to cut off our tails to share your bad luck.

Readers 1, 2, 3 and 4: Misery loves company.

A Readers Theatre Treasury of Stories · Braun & Braun

An African Folktale
retold by Carl Braun
for 5 readers & village people

The Clever Turtle

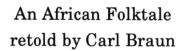

An African Folktale
retold by Carl Braun

Reader 1: A long, long time ago, in far-off Angola a man went to work in his field of maize.

Reader 2: When he got to the field he was shocked.

Reader 3: Where once he had seen beautiful young corn plants, he now saw nothing but broken down stalks.

Reader 1: Among the broken stalks he saw a large turtle dozing in the hot sun.

Reader 2: Immediately he caught the turtle and carried it back to the village.

Reader 3: As soon as he came to the village he called,

Man: What shall we do with this turtle? It has crushed my corn.

Reader 1: The people answered,

Village People: *Punish it! Punish the beast!* That's what we should do.

Man: Tell me, how should we punish the turtle?

Village People: Make turtle stew out of him. That's what we can do.

Reader 2: The man agreed that making turtle stew was a good way to punish the turtle.

Reader 3: When the turtle heard this, she said,

Turtle:	What an excellent idea! I would make a very tasty stew. Just please don't throw me into the river.
Man:	This turtle is not afraid of fire. What else can we do?
Reader 1:	The people said,
Village People:	Tie her to the nearest tree. That's what we can do.
Turtle:	What an excellent idea! Tie me to the nearest tree. Just please, please, **_please_**, don't throw me into the river.
Man:	This turtle is not afraid of fire, and she is not afraid of rope. What else can we do?
Reader 2:	The people said,
Village People:	Make a hole in the ground and put her into the hole.
Turtle:	What an excellent idea! Be sure to dig the hole deep enough so I can't climb out.
Man:	This turtle is not afraid of fire. She is not afraid of rope. This turtle is not afraid of a deep, dark hole. Now, what can we do?
Reader 3:	The people said,
Village People:	Throw her into the river!
Reader 1:	The turtle cried out,
Turtle:	**_No! Please! No!_** Not the river. That river will be the end of me!

Reader 2: So the people carried the large turtle to the river bank.

Reader 3: With a wild heave and a ho, they tossed the turtle as far as they could into the deepest part of the river.

Reader 1: They thought to themselves,

Reader 2: Well, finally we're rid of that pesky turtle.

Reader 3: No sooner had they thought this when,

Reader 1: they saw a whirling and a swirling, and a splattering and a splashing.

Reader 2: And up paddled the turtle looking just as pleased as could be.

Man: I think the turtle has tricked us,

Reader 3: said the man.

Reader 1: And in chorus, the village people shouted,

Village People: That turtle has tricked us. What fools we have been!

Turtle: Born and bred in a river bed,
As you can plainly see.
Whatever you'll try, I'm much too sly,
You'll never get rid of me!

Reader 2: With a grin from one side of the mouth to the other, the clever turtle swam away,

Reader 3: And she was never seen near the village again.

A Readers Theatre Treasury of Stories Braun &Braun

Noise and More Noise

retold by Win Braun
for 8 readers & animals

retold by Win Braun

Reader 1:   Long, long ago, in a faraway land, lived an old man.

Reader 2:   His name was Joshua,

Reader 3:   and he lived in an old house,

Reader 4:   a very old house.

Reader 5:   His rocker creaked.

Reader 6:   C-r-r-rick, cr-r-rack. . .

Reader 1:   The door hinges squeaked,

Reader 2:   **E-e-e-k.**

Reader 3:   The fire crackled,

Reader 4:   **Snap, crack, s-s-s-s. . .**

Reader 5:   An owl hooted in the woods,

Reader 6:   **Twit-t-whoooo. . .**

Reader 1:   Branches brushed the window,

Reader 2:   *Scritch, scratch. . .*

Joshua: So much noise,

Reader 3:   said Joshua.

Reader 4:   He sat on his rocker and thought.

Reader 5:   C-r-r-rick, cr-r-rack. . .

Reader 6:   And thought.

Reader 1:   Joshua decided to see the old sage in the mountains.

Reader 2:   Surely she would know what to do.

Joshua: What can I do?

Reader 3:   Joshua asked the sage.

Joshua:	My house makes so much noise.
	My rocker creaks.
	C-r-r-rick, cr-r-rack. . .
	The door hinges squeak,
	E-e-e-k.
	The fire crackles,
	Snap, crack, s-s-s-s. . .
	An owl hoots in the woods,
	Twit-t-whoooo. . .
	Branches brush the window,
	Scritch, scratch. . .
Sage:	I can help you,
Reader 4:	said the old sage,
Sage:	I know exactly what to do.
Joshua:	What?
Reader 5:	asked Joshua.
Sage:	Get a pig,
Reader 2:	said the old sage of the mountains.
Joshua:	A pig! What good can a pig be?
Reader 3:	But Joshua went to get a pig.
Reader 4:	The pig said,
Pig:	**Oink! Oink! Oink!**
Reader 5:	Joshua was not happy.
Joshua:	My house is still noisy.
	My rocker creaks.
	C-r-r-rick, cr-r-rack. . .
	The door hinges squeak,
	E-e-e-k.
	The fire crackles,

Snap, crack, s-s-s-s. . .

An owl hoots in the woods,

Twit-t-whoooo. . .

Branches brush the window,

Scritch, scratch. . .

And now I have a pig that goes,

Oink! Oink! Oink!

So much noise,

Reader 6:   said Joshua.

Reader 1:   And he travelled once more to see the sage in the mountains.

Sage: Get a rooster,

Reader 2:   said the old sage.

Joshua: A rooster! What good can a rooster be?

Reader 2:   But Joshua got a rooster.

Reader 3:   The rooster said,

Rooster: *Cock-a-doodle-doo!*

Reader 4:   The pig said,

Pig: **Oink! Oink! Oink!**

Reader 5:   Joshua was not happy.

Joshua: My house is still noisy.

My rocker creaks.

C-r-r-rick, cr-r-rack. . .

The door hinges squeak,

E-e-e-k.

The fire crackles,

Snap, crack, s-s-s-s. . .

An owl hoots in the woods,

Twit-t-whoooo. . .

A Readers Theatre Treasury of Stories

Branches brush the window,

Scritch, scratch. . .

I have a pig that goes,

Oink! Oink! Oink!

And now I have a rooster that goes,

Cock-a-doodle-doo!

So much noise,

Reader 6:   said Joshua.

Reader 1:   Once more he travelled to see the sage in the mountains.

Sage: Get a horse,

Reader 2:   said the old sage.

Joshua: A horse! What good can a horse be?

Reader 3:   But Joshua went to get a horse.

Reader 4:   The horse went,

Horse: ***Neigh! Neighhhh. . .***

Reader 5:   The rooster went,

Rooster: ***Cock-a-doodle-doo!***

Reader 6:   The pig went,

Pig: **Oink! Oink! Oink!**

Reader 1:   Joshua was quite unhappy by this time.

Joshua: My house is still noisy. It is very noisy.

My rocker creaks.

C-r-r-rick, cr-r-rack. . .

The door hinges squeak,

E-e-e-k.

The fire crackles,

Snap, crack, s-s-s-s. . .

An owl hoots in the woods,

Twit-t-whoooo. . .

Branches brush the window,

Scritch, scratch. . .

I have a pig that goes,

Oink! Oink! Oink!

I have a rooster that goes,

Cock-a-doodle-doo!

And now I have a horse that goes,

Neigh! Neighhh. . .

So much noise,

Reader 2: sighed Joshua.

Reader 3: So, again, he travelled to see the sage in the mountains.

Sage: Get a goat,

Reader 4: said the old sage.

Joshua: A goat! What good can a goat be?

Reader 5: But Joshua got a goat.

Reader 6: The goat went,

Goat: **Maa! Maaaaa!**

Reader 1: The horse went,

Horse: **Neigh! Neighhhh. . .**

Reader 2: The rooster went,

Rooster: ***Cock-a-doodle-doo!***

Reader 3: The pig went,

Pig: **Oink! Oink! Oink!**

Reader 4: Now Joshua was very unhappy.

Joshua: My rocker creaks.

C-r-r-rick, cr-r-rack. . .

The door hinges squeak,

E-e-e-k.

The fire crackles,

Snap, crack, s-s-s-s. . .

An owl hoots in the woods,

Twit-t-whoooo. . .

Branches brush the window,

Scritch, scratch. . .

I have a pig that goes,

Oink! Oink! Oink!

I have a rooster that goes,

Cock-a-doodle-doo!

I have a horse that goes,

Neigh! Neighhhh. . .

And now I have a goat that goes,

Maa! Maaaaa!

All day and all night!

Reader 5:	Angry and confused, he went to see the sage in the mountains.
Sage:	Get a flock of geese,
Reader 6:	said the old sage,
Joshua:	A flock of geese!
Reader 1:	exclaimed Joshua.
Sage:	And some ducks,
Reader 2:	said the old sage,
Joshua:	What good will geese and ducks be?
Reader 3:	said Joshua.
Reader 4:	But Joshua got a flock of geese and some ducks.

Reader 5:	The geese went,
Geese:	**Honk! Honk! Honk! Honk!**
Reader 6:	The ducks went,
Ducks:	**Quack! Quack! Quack!**
Reader 1:	The goat went,

Goat:	**Maa! Maaaaa!**
Reader 2:	The horse went,
Horse:	**Neigh! Neighhhh. . .**
Reader 3:	The rooster went,
Rooster:	*Cock-a-doodle-doo!*
Reader 4:	The pig went,
Pig:	**Oink! Oink! Oink!**

Reader 5:	Now Joshua was very angry.
Reader 6:	He ran all the way into the mountains to see the old sage.
Joshua:	I told you my house was too noisy,
Reader 1:	he said.
Joshua:	I told you my rocker creaks.
	C-r-r-rick, cr-r-rack. . .
	I told you the door hinges squeak,
	E-e-e-k.
	I told you the fire crackles,
	Snap, crack, s-s-s-s. . .
	I told you the owl hoots in the woods,
	Twit-t-whoooo. . .
	I told you branches brush the window,
	Scritch, scratch. . .
	You told me to get a pig.
	The pig goes **Oink! Oink! Oink!** all day long.
	You told me to get a rooster.
	The rooster goes *Cock-a-doodle-doo!* all day and all night.
	You told me to get a horse.
	The horse goes **Neigh! Neighhhh. . .** all day long.
	You told me to get a goat.
	The goat goes **Maa! Maaaaa!** all day and all night.
	You told me to get a flock of geese.

And ducks.

The geese go **Honk! Honk! Honk! Honk!** all day long.

And the ducks go **Quack! Quack! Quack!** all day and all night.

Joshua:	My house is so noisy! I am going crazy!
Reader 2:	shouted Joshua.
Reader 3:	The old sage said,
Sage:	Do as I tell you.
	Let the pig go.
	Let the rooster go.
	Let the horse go.
	Let the goat go.
	Let the flock of geese go.
	Let the ducks go, too.

Reader 1:	So Joshua let the pig go.
Reader 2:	He let the rooster go.
Reader 3:	He let the horse go.
Reader 4:	He let the goat go.
Reader 5:	He let the flock of geese
Reader 6:	and the ducks go.

Reader 1:	Now no pig said,
Pig:	**Oink! Oink! Oink!**
Reader 2:	Now no rooster said,
Rooster:	*Cock-a-doodle-doo!*
Reader 3:	Now no horse said,
Horse:	**Neigh! Neighhhh...**
Reader 4:	Now no goat said,
Goat:	**Maa! Maaaaa!**
Reader 5:	Now no geese said,

Geese:	**Honk! Honk! Honk! Honk!**
Reader 6:	And no ducks said,
Ducks:	**Quack! Quack! Quack!**
Reader 1:	The rocker creaked.
Joshua:	Ahhhh!
Reader 2:	yawned Joshua,
Joshua:	What a quiet noise!
Reader 3:	The door hinges squeaked.
Joshua:	Ahhhh!
Reader 4:	yawned Joshua.
Joshua:	What a quiet noise!
Reader 5:	An owl hooted in the woods.
Reader 6:	**Twit-t-whoooo. . .**
Joshua:	Ahhhh!
Reader 1:	yawned Joshua,
Joshua:	What a quiet, peaceful noise!
Reader 2:	The fire crackled,
Reader 3:	**Snap, crack, s-s-s-s. . .**
Joshua:	Ahhhh! Ahhhh...
Reader 4:	yawned Joshua in the quietest yawn you could imagine,
Reader 5:	and you could just barely hear him say in the quietest voice,
Joshua:	This house. . .is. . . *sooo* quiet. . .
Reader 6:	And Joshua began to snore. . .
Reader 1:	and dreamed a very quiet dream.

A Readers Theatre Treasury of Stories   Braun &Braun

The Enormous Turnip

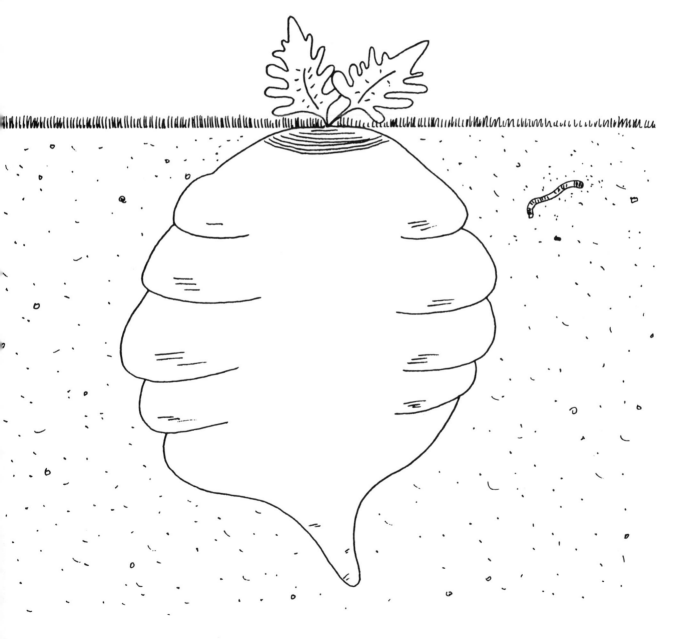

THE ENORMOUS TURNIP

retold by Carl Braun

Reader 1: A very long time ago a little old man and a little old woman planted some turnip seeds.

Reader 2: It didn't take long for the turnips to sprout,

Reader 3: and it wasn't long before the whole garden looked like a sea of turnips.

Reader 4: One day as the little old man and the little old woman looked from their cottage window they saw the strangest sight.

Little Old Man: Do you see what I see?

Reader 1: said the little old man to the little old woman.

Reader 2: The little old woman, indeed, saw what the little old man saw.

Little Old Woman: It is an **ENORMOUS** turnip!

Reader 3: There among all those turnips, one stood out above all the other turnips.

Reader 4: It was the biggest turnip the little old man and the little old woman had ever seen.

Reader 1: The turnip kept **growing** and **growing**.

Reader 2: It grew **bigger**

Reader 3: and **bigger**

Reader4: and **bigger**.

All: It **WAS ENORMOUS!**

Reader 1: One day the little old man said to the little old woman,

Little Old Man: That **enormous** turnip would make a mighty fine soup.

Reader 2:   And off he went to the garden to pull up the **enormous** turnip.

Reader 1:   With a pull and a tug,

Reader 2:   In his heels he dug.

Reader 3:   A **click** and a **cluck**,

Reader 4:   The turnip was stuck.

Reader 3:   The little old man called out to the little old woman,

Little Old Man: Help, help, the turnip is stuck.

Reader4:   The little old woman stood behind the little old man and clasped her arms around the little old man's round belly as

Reader 1:   With a pull and a tug,

Reader 2:   In their heels they dug.

Reader 3:   A **click** and a **cluck**,

Reader 4:   The turnip was stuck.

Reader 1:   The little old woman called out to a little boy,

Little Old Woman: Help, help, the turnip is stuck.

Reader 2:   The little boy held on to the little old woman.

Reader 3:   The little old woman held on to the little old man as

Reader 1:   With a pull and a tug

Reader 2:   In their heels they dug.

Reader 3:   A **click** and a **cluck**,

Reader 4:   The turnip was stuck.

Reader 1:   The little boy called out to a little girl,

Little Boy: Help, help, the turnip is stuck.

Reader 2: The little girl held on to the little boy,

Reader 3: The little boy held on to the little old woman,

Reader 4: And the little old woman held on to the little old man as

Reader 1: With a pull and a tug,

Reader 2:   In their heels they dug.

Reader 3:   With a **click** and a **cluck**,

Reader 4:   **STILL** the turnip was stuck.

Reader 1: The little girl called out to a spotted dog,

Little Girl: Help, help, the turnip is stuck.

Reader 2: The spotted dog held on to the little girl,

Reader 3: The little girl held on to the little boy,

Reader 4: The little boy held on to the little old woman,

Reader 3: And the little old woman held on to the little old man as

Reader 1: With a pull and a tug,

Reader 2:   In their heels they dug.

Reader 3:   With a **click** and a **cluck**.

Readers 1, 2, 3 and 4: **STILL THE TURNIP WAS STUCK**.

Reader 1: The spotted dog called out to a stripy cat,

Spotted Dog: Help, help, the turnip is stuck.

Reader 2: The stripy cat held on to the spotted dog,

Reader 3: The spotted dog held on to the little girl,

Reader 4: The little girl held on to the little boy,

Reader 1: The little boy held on to the little old woman,

Reader 2: And the little old woman held on to the little old man as

Readers 1, 2, 3 and 4:   With a pull and a tug,

                In their heels they dug.

                   With a **click** and a **cluck**,

                      The turnip was stuck.

A Readers Theatre Treasury of Stories

Reader 3: The stripy cat called out to a little grey mouse,

Stripy Cat: Help, help, the turnip is stuck.

Reader 4: The little grey mouse was so pleased and proud to be asked for help.

Reader 1: She puffed out her chest,

Reader 2: and held on to the stripy cat's tail between her tiny paws.

Reader 3: The stripy cat held on to the spotted dog,

Reader 4: The spotted dog held on to the little girl,

Reader 1: The little girl held on to the little boy,

Reader 2: The little boy held on to the little old woman,

Reader 3: And the little old woman held on to the little old man as

Readers 1, 2, 3 and 4: With a pull and a tug,
With a **click** and **cluck**,
The little grey mouse
Brought them luck.

Reader 1: Sure enough, the turnip came out so suddenly that they all fell over backwards,

Reader 2: while the **ENORMOUS** turnip landed on top of them all.

Reader 3: Quickly they helped each other up and brushed off the dirt.

Reader 4: They scrubbed the **ENORMOUS** turnip,

Reader 1: chopped it up,

Reader 2: put it into an **ENORMOUS** pot,

All: and cooked an **ENORMOUS** soup.

The Yellow Ribbon

by Maria Leach
for 5 readers

THE YELLOW RIBBON

by Maria Leach

Reader 1:   John loved Jane.

Reader 2:   They lived next door to each other,

Reader 3:   and they went to first grade together,

Reader 1:   and John loved Jane very much.

Reader 2:   Jane wore a yellow ribbon around her neck every day.

Reader 3:   One day John said,

John: Why do you wear the yellow ribbon?

Jane: I can't tell,

Reader 1:   said Jane.

Reader 2:   But John kept asking, and finally Jane said maybe she'd tell him later.

Reader 3:   The next year they were in the second grade.

Reader 1:   One day John asked again,

John: Why do you wear the yellow ribbon around your neck?

Reader 2:   And Jane said, maybe she'd tell him later.

Reader 3:   Time went by,

Reader 1:   and every once in a while John asked Jane why she wore the yellow ribbon,

Reader 2:   but Jane never told.

Reader 3:   So time went by.

Reader 1:   John and Jane went through high school together.

Reader 2:   They loved each other very much.

Reader 3:   On graduation day John asked Jane,

John:	Please, tell me why you always wear that yellow ribbon around your neck.
Reader 1:	But Jane said, there was no point in telling on graduation day.
Reader 2:	So, she didn't tell.
Reader 3:	Time went by,
Reader 1:	and John and Jane became engaged,
Reader 2:	and finally Jane said, maybe she would tell him on their wedding day.
Reader 3:	The wedding day came, and John forgot to ask.
Reader 1:	But the next day John asked,
John:	Jane, why *are* you wearing that yellow ribbon?
Reader 2:	Jane said,
Jane:	Well, we are happily married, and we love each other, so what difference does it make?
Reader 3:	So John let it pass, but he still *did* want to know.
Reader 1:	Time went by,
Reader 2:	and finally, on their golden wedding anniversary John asked again.
Reader 3:	And Jane said,
Jane:	Since you have waited this long, you can wait a little longer.
Reader 1:	Finally, Jane was taken very ill,
Reader 2:	and when she was dying, John asked again, between sobs,
John:	*Please,* tell me why you wear the yellow ribbon around your neck.
Jane:	All right,
Reader 3:	said Jane,
Jane:	you can untie it now.
Reader 1:	So John untied the yellow ribbon,

Readers 1, 2 and 3:   AND JANE'S HEAD FELL OFF.

A Readers Theatre Treasury of Stories

Wait Till Martin Comes

by Maria Leach
for 9 readers

by Maria Leach

Reader 1: That big house down the road was haunted. Nobody could live in it.

Reader 2: The door was never locked. But nobody ever went in.

Reader 3: Nobody would even spend a night in it.

Reader 4: Some people had tried, but they all came running out pretty fast.

Reader 1: One night a man was going along that road on his way to the next town.

Reader 2: He saw that the sky was getting black.

Reader 3: *No moon.*

Reader 4: *No stars.*

Reader 1: Big storm coming for sure.

Reader 2: He had a long way to go. He knew he couldn't get home before it poured rain.

Reader 3: So he decided to go in that empty house by the road.

Reader 4: He had heard it was haunted. But shucks! Who believed in ghosts? No such thing.

Reader 1: So he went in. He built himself a nice fire on the big hearth, pulled up a chair, and sat down to read a book.

Reader 2: He could hear the rain beating on the windows.

Reader 3: LIGHTNING FLASHED.

Reader 4: The THUNDER CRACKED around the old building.

Reader 1: But he sat there reading.

Reader 2: Next time he looked up there was a little grey cat sitting on the hearth.

Reader 3: That was all right, he thought. *Cozy*.

Reader 4: He went on reading. The rain went on raining.

Reader 1: Pretty soon he heard the door **creak** and a big black cat came sauntering in.

Reader 2: The first cat looked up. He said,

First Cat: What are we going to do with him?

Second Cat: Wait till Martin comes,

Reader 3: said the other cat.

Reader 4: The man went right on reading.

Reader 1: Pretty soon he heard the door **creak** and another great big black cat, as big as a dog, came in.

First Cat: What are we going to do with him?

Reader 2: said the first cat.

Third Cat: Wait till Martin comes,

Reader 3: said the new cat.

Reader 4: The man was awfully scared by this time, but he kept looking in the book, pretending to read.

Reader 1:   Pretty soon he heard the door ***creak*** and a great big black cat, as big as a calf, came in.

Reader 2:   He stared at the man.

Fourth Cat: Shall we do it now?

Reader 3:   he said to all the cats.

Cats 1, 2, & 3:   Wait till Martin comes,

Reader 4:   said the others.

Reader 1:   The man just leaped out of that chair, and out the window, and down the road.

Man: Tell Martin I couldn't wait!

Reader 2:   he said.

A Readers Theatre Treasury of Stories   Braun & Braun

The Snooks Family

by Harcourt Williams
for 9 readers

by Harcourt Williams

Reader 1:   One night Mr. and Mrs. Snooks were going to bed as usual.

Reader 2:   It so happened that Mrs. Snooks got into bed first, and she said to her husband,

Mrs. Snooks: Please, Mr. Snooks, would you blow the candle out?

Reader 3:   And Mr. Snooks replied,

Mr. Snooks: Certainly, Mrs. Snooks.

Reader 4:   So he picked up the candlestick and began to blow.

Reader 1:   But unfortunately he could only blow by putting his bottom lip over his top lip,

Reader 2:   which meant that his breath went up to the ceiling instead of blowing out the candle flame.

Reader 3:   And he **puffed** and he **puffed** and he **puffed**, but he could not blow it out.

Reader 4:   So Mrs. Snooks said,

Mrs. Snooks: I will do it, my dear,

Reader 1:   and she got out of bed and took the candlestick from her husband and began to blow.

Reader 2:   But unfortunately she could only blow by putting her top lip over her bottom lip,

Reader 3:   so that all her breath went down onto the floor.

Reader 4:   And she **puffed** and she **puffed**, but she could not blow the candle out.

A Readers Theatre Treasury of Stories

Reader 1:	So Mrs. Snooks called their son, John.
Reader 2:	John put on his sky-blue bathrobe and slipped his feet into his rose-coloured slippers and came down into his parents' bedroom.
Mrs. Snooks:	John, dear,
Reader 3:	said Mrs. Snooks,
Mrs. Snooks:	will you please blow out the candle for us?
Reader 4:	And John said,
John:	Certainly, Mum.
Reader 1:	But unfortunately John could only blow out of the right corner of his mouth,
Reader 2:	so that his breath hit the wall of the room instead of the candle.
Reader 3:	And he **puffed** and he **puffed**, but he could not blow out the candle.
Reader 4:	So they all called for his little sister, Ann.
Reader 1:	And little Ann put on her scarlet bathrobe and slipped on her pink slippers and came down to her parents' bedroom.
Mr. Snooks:	Ann, dear,
Reader 2:	said Mr. Snooks,
Mr. Snooks:	will you please blow the candle out for us?
Reader 3:	And Ann said,
Ann:	Certainly, Daddy.
Reader 4:	But unfortunately Ann could only blow out of the left side of her mouth,
Reader 1:	so that all her breath hit the wall instead of the candle.
Reader 2:	And she **puffed** and she **puffed** and she **puffed**, but she could not blow out the candle.

Reader 3:	It was just then that they heard in the street below a heavy, steady tread coming along the pavement.
Reader 4:	Mr. Snooks threw open the window and they all craned their heads out.
Reader 1:	They saw a policeman coming slowly towards the house.
Mrs. Snooks:	Oh, Mr. Policeman,
Reader 2:	said Mrs. Snooks,
Mrs. Snooks:	will you come up and blow out our candle? We do so want to go to bed.
Policeman:	Certainly, Madam,
Reader 3:	replied the policeman,
Reader 4:	and he entered and climbed the stairs,
All:	**blump, blump, blump.**

Reader 1:	He came into the bedroom where Mr. Snooks, Mrs. Snooks, John Snooks and little Ann Snooks were standing around the candle which they could **NOT** blow out.
Reader 2:	The policeman then picked up the candlestick in a very dignified manner and,
Reader 3:	putting his mouth into the usual shape for blowing, **puffed** out the candle at the first puff.
Reader 4:	Just like this —
All:	**PUFF!**

Reader 1:	Then the Snooks family all said,
Snooks:	Thank you, Mr. Policeman.
Reader 2:	And the policeman said,
Policeman:	Don't mention it,
Reader 3:	and turned to go down the stairs again.

Mr. Snooks:	Just a moment, Mr. Policeman,
Reader 4:	said Mr. Snooks.
Mr. Snooks:	You mustn't go down the stairs in the dark. You might fall.
Reader 1:	And taking a box of matches,

All:	**HE LIT THE CANDLE AGAIN!**
Reader 2:	Mr. Snooks went down the stairs with the policeman and saw him out of the door.
Reader 3:	His footsteps went
All:	**blump, blump, blump,**
Reader 4:	along the quiet street.

Reader 1:	John Snooks and Ann Snooks went back to bed.
Reader 2:	Mr. and Mrs. Snooks got into bed again.

Reader 3:	There was silence for a moment.
Mrs. Snooks:	Mr. Snooks,
Reader 4:	said Mrs. Snooks,
Mrs. Snooks:	would you blow out the candle?
Reader 1:	Mr. Snooks got out of bed.
Mr. Snooks:	Certainly, Mrs. Snooks,
Reader 2:	he said.

All:	*And so on...and on...and on...*

Appears in unscripted form in C. Braun and P. Goepfert, (1989) *Every Time I Climb A Tree,* Nelson Canada, and McDougall Littell (US)

by Alvin Schwartz
for 4 readers

The Viper

by Alvin Schwartz

Reader 1: A widow lived alone on the top of an apartment house. One morning the telephone rang.

Widow: Hello,

Reader 2: she said.

Viper: **This is the viper,**

Reader 1: a man said.

Viper: **I'm coming up.**

Widow: *Somebody is fooling around,*

Reader 2: the woman thought, and hung up.

Reader 1: A half hour later the telephone rang again. It was the same man.

Viper: **It's the viper,**

Reader 2: he said.

Viper: **I'll be up soon.**

Reader 1: The widow didn't know what to think, but she was getting frightened.

Reader 2: Once more the telephone rang. Again it was the viper.

Viper: **I'm coming up now,**

Reader 1: he said.

Reader 2: The widow quickly called the police. They said they would be right over.

Reader 1: When the doorbell rang, she sighed with relief.
Widow: *They are here!*
Reader 2: she thought.

Reader 1: But when she opened the door, there stood a little old man with a bucket and a cloth.
Viper: **I am the viper,**
Reader 2: he said.
Viper: **I vish to vash and vipe the vindows.**

From: Scary Stories to Tell in The Dark, (1981) New York: Harper and Row Publishers

by Amy Siamon-Rolf von den Baumen
for 4 readers

A Good Walk for Wags

by Amy Siamon-Rolf von den Baumen

Reader 1: It was a beautiful fall day and Wags and his family were **finally** going for a walk.

Reader 2: Wags knew it wasn't going to be one of his favourite walks in the woods . . .

Reader 3: It was going to be one of those **new buggy walks** . . .

Reader 4: . . .with the **new** baby.

Reader 1: They started out with Wags on the leash.

Reader 2: Wags hated his leash and he hated to heel,

Reader 3: . . . especially beside this **new** buggy which kept bumping into him.

Reader 4: Wags was excited when they reached the park full of walking trails where he knew they would let him off his leash.

Reader 1: Even if it wasn't a walk in the woods it was still fun to run free.

Reader 2: Wags' nose quivered with delight in the crisp, fresh, fall air.

Reader 3: As Wags bounded along beside his family, he noticed a new smell coming from a small forest of wild apple trees.

Reader 4: Wags looked back at his family,

Reader 1: but they didn't look up to notice him running towards the apple trees.

Reader 2: They were too busy talking baby talk and ga-gooing down into the **new** buggy.

Reader 3: Wags found the smell of the rotting apples littering the ground delicious.

Reader 4: Maybe if he smelled this good his family would notice him.

Reader 1: So Wags rolled and rolled and wiggled and rolled . . .

Reader 2: until the rotten apple smell covered him.

Reader 3: Then Wags bounded back to his family.

Reader 4: But they didn't notice his new smell.

Reader 1: They were too busy talking baby talk and ga-gooing into the **new** buggy.

Reader 2: The family turned up a new trail with Wags bouncing along beside them.

Reader 3: He was desperately trying to get them interested in a game of 'stick.'

Reader 4: But they didn't notice Wags . . .

Reader 1: or his stick.

Reader 2: They were still too busy talking baby talk and ga-gooing into the **new** buggy.

Reader 3: Off to one side of the trail Wags noticed a pile of fresh, green grass clippings.

Reader 4: Rolling in these piles was one of Wags' favourite pastimes . . .

Reader 1: that is, when he had the chance.

Reader 2: You see, usually his family didn't approve of Wags rolling in **anything**.

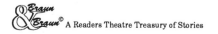

Reader 3: But today they seemed to be very busy with the **new** baby.

Reader 4: Wags took advantage of this rare opportunity.

Reader 1: He rolled and rolled and wiggled and rolled . . .

Reader 2: until he was quite green and his nose was full of grass clippings.

Reader 3: Wags let out a huge sneeze,

Reader 4: but his family didn't hear his big sneeze or notice his new colour.

Reader 1: They were too busy talking baby talk and ga-gooing into the **new** buggy.

Reader 2: Wags chased a squirrel through burr bushes and up a tree.

Reader 3: The burrs stuck his ears in funny directions.

Reader 4: But his family didn't notice his ears.

Reader 1: Wags and his family followed the trail back towards their new subdivision.

Reader 2: "Terrific,"

Reader 3: thought Wags.

Reader 4: He loved the smell of freshly turned red clay they built houses on.

Reader 1: Through the new subdivision Wags ran until his paws were heavy with great globs of red clay.

Reader 2: But . . .

Reader 3: his family didn't notice his heavy feet.

A Readers Theatre Treasury of Stories

Reader 4: Wags found a great muddy, red puddle to bathe in.

Reader 1: He waded in up to his neck and wallowed in the water until he was quite refreshed.

Reader 2: But his family hadn't noticed his bath.

Reader 3: Out of the puddle Wags ran spraying red mud in all directions.

Reader 4: He galloped up to the top of the huge top soil pile and looked down on his family.

Reader 1: But they were **still** talking baby talk and ga-gooing into the **new** buggy.

Reader 2: They didn't notice Wags on top of all that red clay.

Reader 3: Around in big circles Wags ran stirring up great clouds of red dust.

Reader 4: But his family didn't notice it was Wags behind those red clouds.

Reader 1: Down the hill Wags tobogganed on his belly.

Reader 2: But his family didn't notice him sliding.

Reader 3: At the bottom, Wags rolled and rolled and frolicked and wiggled and rolled until . . .

Reader 4: he was entirely caked in thick, gooey, smelly, red clay.

Reader 1: They noticed.

Reader 2: They didn't talk baby talk . . .

Reader 3: or ga-goo into the **new** buggy.

Reader 4: **WAGS** . . .

Reader 1: they hollered.

Reader 2:   Wags bounded happily to his family so glad they had noticed him.

Reader 3:   Red clay splashed in all directions.

Reader 4:   They were talking 'Wags' talk.

Readers 1 and 4:   "What a smell!"

Readers 2 and 3:   "**Look** at his ears!"

Readers 1 and 4:   "What happened to our beautiful golden dog?"

All: "Good Grief! He's green under all of this!"

Reader 2:   Wags wagged his tail thrilled with all the attention he was getting.

Reader 3:   He looked into the **new** buggy and the new baby was grinning up at him.

Reader 4:   Wags leaned over the **new** buggy, dripping red clay everywhere . . .

All: and gave that **new** baby a big, slurpy, muddy, smelly kiss.

by Carl Braun
for 10 readers

The Chocolate Chip Cookie Cure

THE CHOCOLATE CHIP COOKIE CURE

by Carl Braun

Reader 1: A family was enjoying a peaceful evening around the fire when Baby broke the silence with a sudden,

Baby: I'm bored.

Reader 2: Baby never kept her boredom a secret for long.

Reader 3: She knew she would get attention,

Reader 4: and soon!

Reader 1: But, just in case, she emitted another,

Baby: I'm BORED!

Reader 2: And this time with more gusto.

Reader 3: Father closed the book he was reading,

Reader 4: got up from his chair, and said,

Father: I'll get your favourite puzzle for you. You like doing puzzles.

Reader 1: Baby always enjoyed putting puzzles together.

Reader 2: Dad returned to his reading.

Reader 3: In no time at all, Baby broke the silence once more,

Baby: I'm bored, really bored!
A puzzle to do,
That's nothing new!
I'm bored!

Reader 4: It was Mother's turn to respond to Baby's call .

Reader 1:	She left her work and picked up Baby's wind-up train from the shelf, and said,
Mother:	Here's your wind-up train. You love playing with your wind-up train.
Reader 2:	Baby always enjoyed playing with her wind-up train.
Reader 3:	Mother returned to her work.
Reader 4:	In no time at all, Baby broke the silence. Her voice was getting louder.

Baby: I'm still bored, really, REALLY bored!

A puzzle to do,

That's nothing new.

My wind-up train?

It drives me insane!

I'm bored!

Reader 1:	Big Brother knew that the family was in for a "Guess What Baby Wants" show.
Reader 2:	He left his homework and walked into the next room.
Reader 3:	He knew what would make Baby happy, maybe...
Reader 4:	He returned with Baby's new truck from Aunt Daisy.
Big Brother:	Here is your new truck from Aunt Daisy.

Reader 1:	And Big Brother went back to his homework.
Reader 2:	Baby hadn't really played with the truck at all when she called louder than ever,

Baby: I'm bored, bored, BORED! Really, really, REALLY bored!

A puzzle to do,

That's nothing new.

My wind-up train?

It drives me insane.

My truck from Aunt Daisy?

Trucks drive me crazy.

I'm bored!

Reader 3: It was Big Sister's turn. She left the project she had just started, and confidently walked over to Baby's room.

Reader 4: She was always able to find just the right thing for Baby. This time she'd try her dolls from Aunt Flore.

Big Sister: Here are the dolls Aunt Flore sent you. You always enjoy playing with your dolls.

Reader 1: And Big Sister returned to work on her project.

Reader 2: Baby did play with her dolls.

Reader 3: But not for long.

Reader 4: With all the force she could muster, she hollered,

Baby: I'm bored! I'm bored! I'm BORED! Do you hear me? I'm BORED!

A puzzle to do,

That's nothing new!

A wind-up train?

It drives me insane!

My truck from Aunt Daisy?

Trucks drive me crazy.

And dolls from Aunt Flore?

They're such a bore.

I'm bored!

Reader 1: Clearly, it was Granny's turn. She was watching her favourite TV show.

Reader 2: She was sure that she'd be able to cure Baby's boredom.

Reader 3: It always worked.

Reader 4: She walked into the kitchen, and appeared with the biggest oatmeal chocolate chip cookie Baby had ever seen.

Reader 1: Granny quietly returned to watch the end of her TV show.

Reader 2: The look on Granny's face as much as said,

Granny: Look, everybody, **I know boredom when I see it! What's more, I know how to cure it.**

Reader 3: And she had.

Reader 4: Baby's attack on the cookie showed every sign of cured boredom.

Reader 1: To make sure that everyone knew that she no longer was bored, she announced loudly,

Baby: I'm NOT bored.
A puzzle to do
That's nothing new!
My wind-up train?
It drives me insane.
My truck from Aunt Daisy?
Trucks drive me crazy.
And dolls from Aunt Flore?
They're such a bore.
As for a snack,
HEAR MY LIPS SMACK.

Reader 2: Father, Mother, Big Brother and Big Sister gasped in a chorus of disbelief,

Father, Mother, Big Brother and Sister:
Why didn't you say you were hungry?

Baby: NOBODY ASKED!

by Eve Bunting
for 5 readers

where's
willie

WHERE'S WILLIE

by Eve Bunting

Narrator: We have a chameleon. His name is Willie. Sometimes people who don't know any better call him a lizard. But he's a chameleon.

Mom likes Willie a lot. She made a home for him in an old fishbowl filled with dirt, rocks, and a stick for Willie to climb. But Willie would rather be out, skittering around the house. Willie is very independent.

My sister Keke and I like Willie a lot, too. It's fun to play hide-and-seek with him. Willie hides and we seek. Willie changes his colour to match what he's lying on. When he's on our green couch, Willie's green. When he's on our brown rug, Willie's brown. He's rust red on the pillow and a lighter , newer green when he roosts in Mother's fern.

Dad doesn't like Willie at all. That's because once he almost sat on Willie, once he almost stood on him, and once he almost *lay* on him when Willie got into Dad's bed. Yellow sheets and yellow Willie.

Dad: Keep that lousy lizard out of my bed,
Narrator: Dad yelled.
Mom: He's not a lizard, he's a chameleon,
Narrator: Mom said.
Dad: He's a pest,
Narrator: Dad told her.

Dad's an artist, and he's always careful to keep his studio door closed — because of Willie. And because Dad gets mad, we're careful to keep the door closed, too.

One evening Dad was bringing home a customer whose name was Mr. Rich. Mr. Rich had built a bunch of houses outside of town, and he wanted Dad to do an advertisement for him. You might think Mr. Rich's name is a joke. It isn't; it's his real name and it suits him because he is, in fact, rich. If Dad sells him art for his billboards, we will be sort of rich, too.

Mom had made Mandarin tea and her yummy Pagoda Friendship cake to sweeten up Mr. Rich, and Keke and I had tidied the house and ourselves. We were all ready when Keke suddenly said,

Keke: Where's Willie?

Narrator: Mom went

Mom: Hssss

Narrator: and rolled her eyes.

Mom: Where *is* Willie?

Narrator: He wasn't up in the lamp, where he likes to be because it's warm. He wasn't inside the morning newspaper, where he likes to be because it's dark. And he wasn't in the avocado plant, where he likes to be because sometimes there are juicy bugs clinging under the leaves.

Mom: Oh, dear,

Narrator: Mom said,

Mom: Here's Jim.

Narrator: Jim is Dad.

Mom: Not a word about Willie, girls,

Narrator: she warned.

Mom: But seek, girls, seek.

Narrator: Keke and I knew what she meant.

Mom, Dad and Mr. Rich sat at the kitchen table and had Mandarin tea and Pagoda Friendship cake. Mr. Rich had three pieces, which certainly must have sweetened him up. Before they sat down, Keke and I ran our hands all over their chairs, seeking Willie. Safe! We patted the couch before Mr. Rich sank into it. Safe! And when Mr. Rich stood and said,

Mr. Rich: Well now, how about a look at your poster, Jim,

Narrator: Keke and I scampered ahead of him on the stairs, seeking on each step.

Mr. Rich: Lively little girls you have there,

Narrator: Mr. Rich said. He looked a little taken aback. Since we're half Chinese, he probably thought sweeping the stairs in front of guests was some ancient Chinese custom.

Keke: Uh — oh,

Narrator: Keke said as she looked at Dad's studio door. It was open, and it was my fault because I'd tidied the studio.

We slipped in behind Dad and Mr. Rich. "Seek," I whispered to Keke. We could see right away that Willie wasn't on the floor. The floor is wood. Willie shows up on it like a lump on a log.

Dad has one easy chair. It's soft and squashy and green... Willie's kind of chair, and Mr. Rich was heading straight for it. I scuttled ahead of him, stroking the cushions, running my hands over the arms.

A Readers Theatre Treasury of Stories

Mr. Rich: Charming! Charming!

Narrator: Mr. Rich had a dazed look as he settled in the chair. He'd have been more dazed if he'd sat on Willie. Not to mention how dazed Willie would have been.

Dad was giving us one of his famous piercing glances. He knew what was going on. Willie would get it after this. I would, too.

Dad: Well,

Narrator: Dad said.

Dad: Would you like to come over to my drawing table, Mr. Rich?

Narrator: Mr. Rich lifted himself up and ambled across. Keke and I walked in front of him, seeking desperately. Dad's oversized watercolour was spread on his big table. Keke went,

Keke: Hsss!

Narrator: and put her hands over her mouth.

Keke gets her hsssing from Mother. I looked at the poster and wanted to hsss myself.

Dad: I think this says what needs to be said about your new development,

Narrator: Dad said, and he read out loud,

Dad: Make the Change to Rich Homes. You'll Blend Right In.

Narrator: That was the slogan he'd printed at the top of the poster. Underneath were the red-roofed houses, the blue lake, the green golf course — and a chameleon spread out by the first tee. A shaft of late sunlight lay warm on Willie's shiny, grass-green back.

A Readers Theatre Treasury of Stories Braun & Braun

"He's asleep," I whispered to Keke.

Mr. Rich: Clever! Clever!

Narrator: Mr. Rich said, and Dad looked bewildered because, let's face it, he hadn't done anything clever. The painting was pretty, sure. But the words were kind of dumb.

Mr. Rich: I like it, I like it,

Narrator: Mr. Rich said.

"He likes it, he likes it," I whispered to Keke.

Mr. Rich: A nice touch, that — putting in the kind of lizard that changes colour.

Narrator: "He's a chameleon," I said.

Dad jerked his head round at Willie and then at us.

Dad: Hsss!

Narrator: he said. He's picked up Mom's hsssing, too. Then Dad realized that Mr. Rich was smiling and rubbing his hands together.

Mr. Rich: You'll blend right in! A little humour there. Humour sells houses,

Narrator: Mr. Rich boomed.

Dad: It does?

Narrator: Dad boomed back. I hoped all this booming wouldn't waken Willie.

Mr. Rich: Papier-mache, is it? Plastic?

Narrator: Mr. Rich was leaning forward, one arm outstretched.

Dad: Don't touch,

Narrator: Dad said quickly,

Dad: It's. . . it's. . .

Narrator: "It's still soft," I said. I'm good at not lying.

Mr. Rich: Well, I'm sold, I'm sold.

Narrator: Mr. Rich was turning away.

Mr. Rich: Come to my office tomorrow, Jim, and we'll sign on the deal.

Narrator: As soon as he and Dad disappeared, I picked up Willie. He immediately spat and turned yellow, which he does when he's mad. Willie hates to be disturbed.

So Dad sold his art, and now the posters with their fake chameleons are all over town: *CHAMELEON HOMES. YOU'LL BLEND RIGHT IN.*

You'd think Dad would like Willie now after what Willie did for him. Dad doesn't say. But every time he goes out he brings home mealworms for Willie, which is nice, because mealworms are Willie's most favourite thing in the whole world. But Willie won't eat them if Dad's looking. Willie is very independent.

From: Braun, C., P. Goepfert, and S. Siamon, (1989), *Whenever the Wind Is High,* Toronto, Canada: Nelson Canada

A Readers Theatre Treasury of Stories

The Snake on 2ⁿᵈ Avenue

by Adele Dueck
for 3 readers

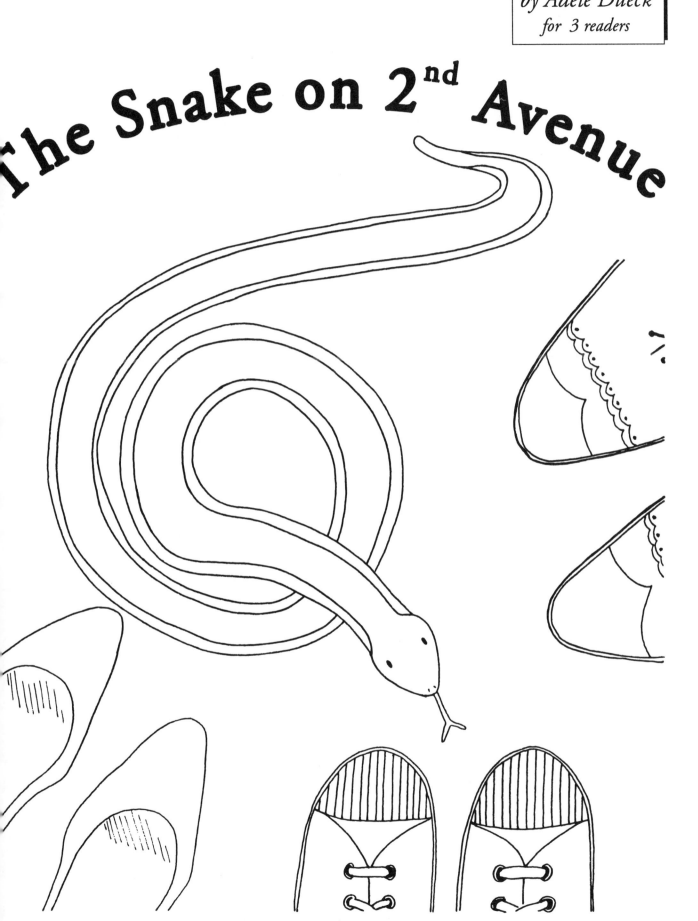

THE SNAKE ON SECOND AVENUE

by Adele Dueck

Narrator: It wasn't my idea to have a snake for a pet. I don't like animals much, and as far as wild animals go — well, cats are too wild for me. But my mother's batty about animals. She watches nature shows on TV and writes letters to the editor complaining about inhumane traps. I find it a little tiresome, but mostly Mum's all right. She never complains when she has to pick me up after ball practice, even though she thinks I should be bird-watching instead.

We were in Saskatoon for a dentist appointment the day we found the snake. It was a little garter snake, the kind we have in the garden at home — green with yellow stripes. There was one thing unusual about this one, though. It was on Second Avenue right outside a shoe store. The snake looked really scared and I don't blame it. It was too small to be made into shoes, but that wasn't its biggest worry. From the look of the crowd gathered around it on the sidewalk, the busy street would have been safer.

We noticed the crowd from the end of the block. As we got closer we could hear a kid scream over and over,

Kid: Kill it ! Kill it!

Narrator: I don't know why the kid didn't just leave. As soon as Mum heard the kid yell she doubled her speed. I ran along with her because I was pretty curious about what all the people were staring at. A mouse? A Martian? A kid playing hooky?

A Readers Theatre Treasury of Stories

Mum pushed her way through the crowd and I followed. The snake was coiled up on the sidewalk. Everyone seemed to be arguing about how to kill it.

Mum: **Oh, poor thing!**

Narrator: exclaimed Mum. She went straight to the snake and picked it up. It was already so frightened that it didn't even try to get away. It just wrapped its tail around her wrist and poked its tongue in and out.

There was a horrified silence. Even the kill-it kid stopped yelling.

Mum: **It's just a garter snake,**

Narrator: said Mum quite loudly.

Mum: It's not poisonous and it's not a constrictor. The only things it can damage are insects.

Narrator: She paused, then said,

Mum: And I'm going to take it home. Please excuse me.

Narrator: She didn't have to push her way out. The crowd just separated in front of her. She seemed to have forgotten me so I followed along behind, watching the snake move in her hands and wondering what it felt like. We'd reached the car before I noticed where we were. "Hey, Mum," I exclaimed, "I thought we were going to buy me some jeans."

Mum: With a snake?

Narrator: she asked.

Mum: We're going home now. You'll have to hold the snake.

Narrator: I wish she'd waited till we were in the car. I don't want you to think I'm chicken, but the first time I hold a snake, I'd like advance warning.

Terrified that I might drop it, I just blinked and grabbed the thing around the neck. I was surprised at how it felt — not slimy at all, but hard and dry on the top and soft underneath. Its head was amazingly small, but it still kept sticking its tongue out. I stuck mine out at it, then climbed into the car.

Mum started the engine and said,

Mum: I've heard that garter snakes make good pets.

Narrator: I groaned, but I knew there was no point in arguing. And really, it wasn't so bad. I could probably write a science report on it and amaze all the teachers. After all, there are worse things than living in the same house with a snake. At least it wasn't a cat.

Appears in unscripted form in: C. Braun and P. Goepfert, *Strategies: Swinging Below A Star*, (1989),(Toronto: Nelson Canada) and McDougall Littell (US)

by Carl Braun
for 4 readers & voices

Super Kid Blues

SUPER KID BLUES

by Carl Braun

Super Kid: I think of myself as a kind of normal kid. I'm not brainy; I'm not stupid. I'm not especially good-looking; I'm not an ugly duckling. I'm seldom cantankerous; I'm not a shrinking violet. I'm not first when it comes to games; I'm seldom last.

I'm not the most energetic person on the planet; I'm not what other normal people would call lazy. Doesn't that sound like a normal kid? You should hear my family, and you'd think I was anything but normal. They would like me to be **Super Kid**.

I'm supposed to be super chore person around the house. I'm supposed to look like **Super Kid** before I leave the house. I'm supposed to be Mr. Super Guy when it comes to having my homework done.

Two or Three Voices: Neat, and tidy, and correct, **HEAR**?

Super Kid: So just for once I fool myself into thinking that I'll just get dressed like a normal kid, slip into my place for breakfast without being noticed and just start the day like a normal kid. Well! Before she even says, "Hi, Joe, did you have a good rest," or something civilized like that, Mom starts on one of her **DID YOU** recitals.

Mom: DID YOU. . .

  A Readers Theatre Treasury of Stories

Remember to straighten your room

Make your bed

See that the goldfish are properly fed?

Flush the toilet

Scrub the sinks

Take out the garbage before it stinks?

Super Kid: And she can ask all those questions without even looking at me, even coming up for air. And how can I answer six questions with one "yes" or "no"? As for straightening my room, I think the room's just fine, but what **I** think doesn't matter. For what it's worth, I think the answer is neither "yes" nor "no." If I want to be fair about it, the answer would be "sort of". I did make my bed. So the answer is partly "yes." I think the goldfish are properly fed. So that's another "yes." I have flushed the toilet since I was two, so it's plain silly to ask the question. But it's a "yes" if the question has to pass. I did not scrub the sinks. That's Steve's job. The answer is "no." I have not taken out the garbage. But there is nothing in the garbage that could possibly stink. So I don't know how to answer that one. I'm still deciding how I should answer all those questions, when Mom opens fire on another six. She likes things in sixes.

And she starts in the predictable,

Mom: **DID YOU. . .**

Button your shirt

Do up your laces

Zip up your pants in appropriate places?

> Brush your teeth
>
>> Blow your nose
>>
>>> Check for dirt between your toes?

Super Kid: This is the "Are you fit to be seen on the street?" set of questions. This time I don't even stop to think. I'm too annoyed, partly because of the questions, but also because of the zipper hang up she has. Appropriate places! The pants I usually wear have only one zipper, and that zipper is there to zip up the fly. But Mom doesn't want to say that word. Fly! Is that a naughty word, or what? I don't know what to think. Most normal kids wouldn't have to put up with this stuff. But there's more. Dad will never miss a turn. He uses Mom's **DID YOU** approach.

Dad: **DID YOU...**
> Walk the dog
>
>> Go to the dairy
>>
>>> Check the feed for your new pet canary?
>
> Do your math
>
>> Practice your spelling
>>
>>> Clean the kennel to keep it from smelling?

Super Kid: These questions are even worse than Mom's. As for answers. There may be a "yes"; clearly some "no's"; at least one "who cares," and a "not on your life," although, I would never say that to Dad. I would have to endure the "When I Was Your Age" lecture. Well, no thanks! Dad actually is expecting an answer. His questions are never just routine. I am thinking! I am thinking! But not for long. Jeannie, my older sister, comes with her "hurry up" look which means

A Readers Theatre Treasury of Stories

that it's time to get off to school. And she doesn't like being late. She is the original "Have you...? police woman. She wants me to be **Super Kid** in school because I'm her brother. She would like me to be just like her. So before I'm even poised for attack, she goes, **HAVE YOU**. . .? She does not copy Mom and Dad's **DID YOU** routine. To copy Mom and Dad isn't exactly cool, so – this morning it's,

Jeannie: **HAVE YOU...**

    Got your sneakers

        Your library book,

            Quickly take a final look.

    Got your mittens

        Packed your lunch

            You've forgotten something, I have a hunch.

Super Kid: Mom and Dad just sit there and let her boss me. Well, I've had enough. My answers come to me in a flash, and I begin.

I DID . . .

    All my homework

        More than enough

            I've cleaned, I've straightened, and all that stuff.

I HAVE . . .

    Dusted, I've mopped, I've wiped, I've cleaned

        I've burped the baby

        I've primped, I've preened.

    I've done my spelling, finished my math,

        There isn't a thing

            To incur teacher's wrath.

I HAVE . . .

> Taken a shower, I've blown my nose,
> Who cares what's lodging
> Between my toes?
> As for the garbage it seldom stinks,
> You know my zipper
> Is missing links.

I HAVE . . .

> Stubbed my toe
> My breakfast is yucky,
> I've scrubbed things clean from here to Kentucky.
> I've lost my keys
> I've broken my laces
> Something's sticking in my braces.

I HAVE . . .

> Done a day's work,
> I'm hardly lazy
> Take a hint, *YOU'RE DRIVING ME CRAZY.*

Now, that feels good. My Mom listens. My Dad listens. Even my sister listens. They just sit there and listen till I'm finished. And then the surprise. As though they've rehearsed what they're going to say, in one loud chorus they exclaim,

Mom, Dad, and Jeannie: Joe, you're a

Super Kid.

Emily's Shadow

by Win Braun
for 4 readers

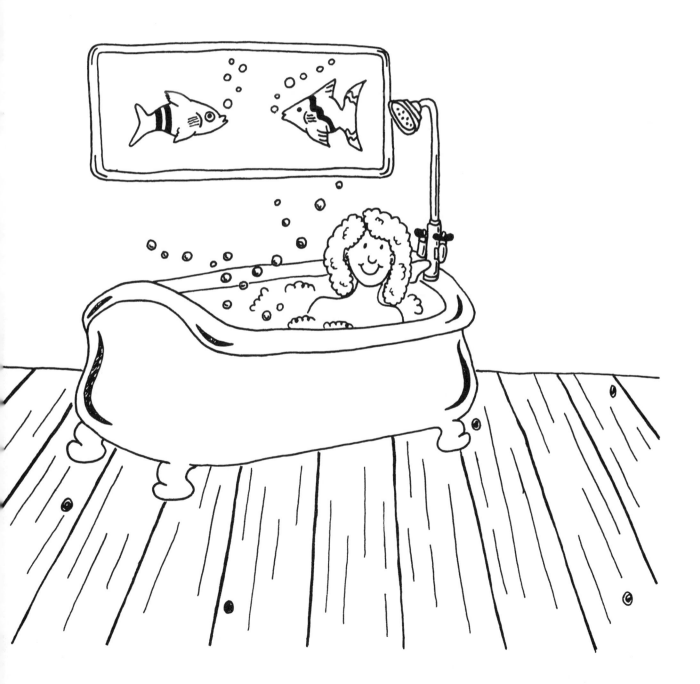

by Win Braun

All: **Scrub! Scrub! Scrub-a-dub-dub!**

Reader 1:   Emily felt so clean! Squeaky, squeaky clean!

Reader 2:   She felt invigorated as she sloshed her way out of the tub.

Reader 1:   Quickly, she dried off (just enough to get by) and wriggled into her clothes as fast as a dripping body will wriggle.

Emily: *No shadow today!*

Reader 2:   Emily yelped as she straddled her bike and took off in the shade of the summer trees, up and down the winding hills, and around the block.

Reader 1:   Emily's triumph did not last long.

All: **Aaaah! Cerunch!**

Reader 2:   *Shadow* had taken one Tarzanic leap from the top of a giant tree, and with one swoop, landed on the bike right behind Emily.

Reader 1:   Emily's bike careened, and she took off down the hill like tumbleweeds in a tornado.

Reader 2:   Emily managed to come to a stop just before the great oak at the bottom of the hill.

Reader 1:   In a rage, Emily turned around to catch a glimpse of a grinning *Shadow* face.

Shadow: How nice to see you again, Emily, and thanks for the ride,

Reader 2:   said *Shadow* in a hollow shadow voice.

Emily: *Shadow*, just go away! Go away, and please don't ever come back,

Reader 1:   fumed Emily.

Reader 2:   *Shadow* smiled the meekest smile as she shrunk just a little. All she could say was,

Shadow: You're my best friend, Emily. You are my only friend. *Please*, don't send me away.

Reader 1:   Like a flash of lightning, Emily took off, sneaking a quick glance over her shoulder. It seemed she had left *Shadow* behind.

Reader 2:   She kept going, wishing for a cloudy day. Somehow, *Shadow* didn't bother her on cloudy days.

Reader 1:   After a while she came to her favourite spot — the river bank where she loved to collect rocks — precious gems to a young pirate like her.

Reader 2:   She bent down to gather the sparkling gems beneath the water's surface.

Reader 1:   Emily reached over to pick up a sparkling blue gem. She couldn't believe her eyes. The precious gem suddenly turned dull. No more sparkling blue shimmering in the water.

Reader 2:   And guess who? *Shadow* was right there. As soon as Emily bent over to pick up a rock, there was *Shadow* reaching just beyond her hand.

Reader 1:   Emily flew into a rage, turned around to flail at her silent assailant. But *Shadow* just ducked this way and that every time Emily moved.

Reader 2:   Emily shouted in disgust,

Emily: To fight with you is like fighting with a cloud. I just wish you would go away. ***Forever!***

Reader 1:   *Shadow* smiled a sad, sheepish smile, and shrunk just a little before she said,

Shadow: I was just trying to help. *Please! Please*, don't send me away!

Reader 2: Emily ignored Shadow's plea, jumped on her bike and rode off as fast as she could.

Reader 1: She had finally come up with a plan. She'd go to the library and find a book that would tell her just how to get rid of shadows. That's what she would do.

Reader 2: No more shadows, ever!

Reader 1: She got to the library, whisked past the librarian over to the walls of books. Books, everywhere!

Emily: Books about shaggy dogs and sheep dogs. Books on sheep sheering. Books about shipbuilding. Heh, now! Books about shadow puppets. Well, almost, but not quite.

Reader 2: Emily kept searching and searching. There were so many books on just about everything. Had no one ever thought about the problem of getting rid of shadows?

Reader 1: Disappointed, Emily finally settled for a book called, *How to Manage the Ghost in Your Life*. At least she might get some ideas!

Reader 2: She found a place near the window and began to read.

Reader 1: She read and read.

Emily: Interesting stuff,

Reader 2: she thought to herself.

Reader 1: She got more and more involved, so involved that she didn't notice a little visitor peering over her shoulder.

Reader 2: It was *Shadow*, and she felt all warm and fuzzy inside to be so close to her favourite person. She just watched Emily read and read.

A Readers Theatre Treasury of Stories Braun & Braun©

Reader 1:   The happier she felt the further she leaned over Emily's shoulder. She leaned over a little too far, far enough to tumble right on to the page.

Reader 2:   Emily emerged from her ghost reverie with a start. She was not pleased. She was angry.

Reader 1:   She said in a most disgusting voice,

Emily: *Shadow*, *Shadow*, disappear!
I don't like you to be near!

Reader 2:   *Shadow* looked at Emily sheepishly. A little tear dropped from her face as she grew smaller and smaller, and then,

All: **POP!**

Reader 1:   *Shadow* was gone.

Emily: Finally! Finally! I'm free! No more *Shadow* stretching when I stretch. No more *Shadow* kicking when I kick. No more *Shadow*!

Reader 2:   Emily looked around just to be sure. She looked behind library books. She even looked under S in the dictionary, just in case. *Shadow* had disappeared. Outside the sun was pushing shadows from trees and buildings.

Reader 1:   But Emily's *Shadow* was nowhere to be seen. How wonderful!

Reader 2:   But standing by her bike Emily saw the meanest looking kid she had ever seen.

Reader 1:   A kid with a scowl, a kid who with just a look said, "Keep your distance!"

Reader 2:   Emily did not like the look of the kid one bit. In fact, she was scared to get to her bike.

Reader 1:   What could she do? She had come all by herself, except, of course, for that nuisance, *Shadow*.

Reader 2:   Emily dragged her feet to the bike and gingerly lifted it from the bike rack.

Reader 1:   But that was enough. The bully put her hand firmly on the bike, and Emily backed off.

Reader 2:   Emily's legs turned into chocolate pudding, legs that would not carry her very far. She just stood there shaking in fear.

Reader 1:   Suddenly, *Shadow* loomed over the mean kid, bigger than Emily had ever known her to be.

Reader 2:   The bully stumbled this way and that, her face as grey as the summer thunder clouds overhead. When the bully finally found her feet, she fled.

Reader 1:   Emily bent over to tie her shoe.

Reader 2:   *Shadow* bent over to tie Emily's shoe.

Emily: Thanks, *Shadow*,

Reader 1:   stammered Emily.

Reader 2:   *Shadow* joined Emily on her ride home. She bounced along on the bumpy parts. She floated along as the bike glided along the smooth parts.

Reader 1:   Shadow's fuzzy feeling returned once again, as Emily sang:

Emily: *Shadow, Shadow*
Stay with me,
We'll be friends,
Just wait and see!

A Readers Theatre Treasury of Stories   Braun & Braun

by Boris Zakhoder
for 10 readers & voices

The Crocodile's Toothbrush

THE CROCODILE'S TOOTHBRUSH

by Boris Zakhoder

Translated by Marguerita Rudolph

Reader 1: Once there was a crocodile who lived in Africa, in a big river.

Reader 2: Now this crocodile was fierce and terrible in every way — which is what you would expect from an honest-to-goodness crocodile.

Reader 3: He had a terrible tail,

Reader 4: a terrible head,

Reader 5: a terrible mouth,

Reader 6: and **VERY TERRIBLE TEETH** which he never brushed.

Reader 1: He did not brush his **TERRIBLE TEETH** either in the morning before breakfast or at night before going to bed.

Reader 2: We must give him credit, though — he never missed taking a bath.

Reader 3: But then, when you live in the river it's not such a trick to take a bath, is it?

Reader 4: So it's not surprising that one fine day Crocodile got a toothache.

Reader 5: And what a toothache!

Reader 6: It was **TERRIBLE**.

Reader 1: Actually only one tooth was hurting, but it seemed to Crocodile that all his teeth were hurting — at the same time.

Reader 2: First there was a pricking and a gnawing sensation,

Reader 3: then it felt as if a drill were going through his teeth,

Reader 4: and then it felt like a gun-shot on top of that !

A Readers Theatre Treasury of Stories · Braun & Braun©

Reader 5:	Crocodile didn't know which way to turn!
Reader 6:	He'd throw himself into the water and dive to the very bottom, hoping that the cool water would ease the pain.
Reader 1:	And it did seem as though he felt better.
Reader 2:	Then the tooth would start gnawing twice as much.
Reader 3:	He was beside himself with pain.
Reader 4:	He jumped out onto the hot sand on the shore, hoping that the heat would help him.
Reader 5:	And it did seem to help.
Reader 6:	But then ...
Reader 1:	He groaned, he grunted, he sniffed
Reader 2:	(some believe those things help),
Reader 3:	but still the pain grew worse.
Reader 4:	But the worst thing of all was that there was no one to feel sorry for him because he was a **TERRIBLE CROCODILE.**
Reader 5:	Only the other week he ate two rabbits and a baby gazelle and he bit off the wing of a parrot.
Reader 6:	Of course, all the animals heard the **TERRIBLE CROCODILE.**
Reader 1:	And the birds and beasts came together from all around.
Reader 2:	They stood a distance away and watched with amazement.
Reader 3:	There was plenty to watch, too, for Crocodile twisted himself and spun around and dashed from side to side and banged his head on the rocks,
Reader 4:	and he even tried jumping on one of his little feet.
Reader 5:	But none of this helped him, not one little bit.
Reader 6:	And to make things worse, his paws were so short that, no matter how hard he tried, he couldn't reach to pick or touch his teeth
Reader 1:	(although even if he could have reached them, it wouldn't have helped him much).

Reader 2: Finally, in desperation, poor Crocodile stretched himself under a big, enormous banana tree

Reader 3: (he couldn't fit under a small one),

Crocodile: **Ouch, ouch, ouch!**

Reader 4: he cried in a bass, a **TERRIBLE** bass voice.

Crocodile: Oh, my poor teeth! **Ouch, ouch, ouch!** Oh, poor me, Crocodile!

Reader 5: Well, that wail proved to be the cause for celebration for the other creatures.

Reader 6: Some of them yelled:

Voices: It serves you right!

Reader 1: And others shouted:

Voices: Aha — you've had it coming. Now you are caught.

Reader 2: The birds were especially amused by the toothache — for they have no teeth at all.

Reader 3: And now Crocodile felt so hurt and humiliated that tears rolled out of his eyes — **TERRIBLY** big tears!

Parrot: Look at that! **Crocodile tears!**

Reader 4: yelled the bright-colored parrot, and he burst into laughter.

Reader 5: Others who knew the meaning of that saying laughed also.

Reader 6: And then everybody else laughed.

Reader 1: They soon raised such a commotion with their noise and laughter that the small bird Tari, a charming white bird with black spots, a little smaller than a peewit, flew down to see what was going on.

Reader 2: And when she found out she became very angry.

Tari: Aren't you ashamed of yourselves?

Reader 3: she called in her clear resonant voice.

A Readers Theatre Treasury of Stories

Reader 4:	Everyone immediately became quiet and then one could hear Crocodile's sighs and groans.
Monkey:	And why should we be ashamed?
Reader 5:	asked one of the monkeys.
Tari:	It's shameful to laugh at poor Crocodile,
Reader 6:	answered the bird Tari.
Tari:	He has a toothache. It hurts him.
Monkey:	One might think YOU know what a toothache or even a tooth is,
Reader 1:	the monkey snickered, making a monkey face.
Tari:	But I know very well what "hurt" means!
Reader 2:	said Tari.
Tari:	I know that if you hurt and someone makes fun of you, you feel twice as bad! You can see — Crocodile is crying!
Parrot:	**Crocodile tears!**
Reader 3:	repeated Parrot with a laugh.
Reader 4:	But no one else laughed.
Tari:	Oh, you Parrot,
Reader 5:	said Tari scornfully.
Tari:	You don't even know what you are talking about. These are not crocodile tears the way YOU mean it— pretend tears!
Parrot:	I don't understand what you mean.
Reader 6:	Parrot was puzzled.
Parrot:	If it's Crocodile who is crying, they are crocodile tears.
Tari:	Oh, YOU,
Reader 1:	said little bird Tari.

Tari:	Don't you think his teeth REALLY hurt? Of course they do! So he is crying with real tears. Real, honest-to-goodness bitter tears.
Crocodile:	They certainly are real,
Reader 2:	Crocodile said in a **TERRIBLE** deep voice, and suddenly he stopped crying.
Crocodile:	**Hey!**
Reader 3:	he said in astonishment.
Crocodile:	It seems that . . . that I feel better now! NO! **Ouch, ouch, ouch!** It only seems that way.
Reader 4:	And he started crying even louder.
Monkey:	Just the same, I am not sorry for him,
Reader 5:	the monkey declared.
Monkey:	It's Crocodile's own fault. Why does he never brush his teeth? He should follow our example.
Reader 6:	And she proceeded to clean his teeth with the bristly twig from a special tree — she was copying tooth-brushing from people.
Crocodile:	But I never . . .
Reader 1:	Crocodile groaned.
Crocodile:	I never knew you have to brush your teeth.
Tari:	But if you had known, would you have brushed them?
Reader 2:	Tari asked.
Crocodile:	If I had known? Of course not,
Reader 3:	Crocodile sniffled.
Crocodile:	How can I brush my teeth when I have such **TERRIBLY** short feet?

Tari:	But what if you could, would you then brush them?
Reader 4:	Tari insisted.
Crocodile:	And how!
Reader 5:	said Crocodile.
Crocodile:	Am I not a clean animal who is accustomed to daily bathing? Although that isn't such a clever thing when one lives in the river,
Reader 6:	he added modestly.
Reader 1:	And right there and then Tari,
Reader 2:	the white bird with black spots, a bird a touch bigger than a dove and a bit smaller than a peewit,
Reader 3:	performed such a marvelous thing that all the creatures simply gaped in wonder.
Reader 4:	She flew bravely right towards Crocodile's **TERRIBLE MOUTH**, right up to his nose, and commanded:
Tari:	Open your mouth!
Reader 5:	Everybody gasped and moved back a step because Crocodile's mouth —
Reader 6:	you haven't forgotten —
Reader 1:	was **TERRIBLE** and it was full of **VERY TERRIBLE TEETH.**
Reader 2:	And now everybody was even more astonished.
Reader 3:	Some screamed from fear and some closed their eyes when they saw the bird Tari hop right into the Crocodile's mouth.
Tari:	Watch out, don't decide to close your mouth, or else this won't work for either of us,
Reader 4:	she said.
Reader 5:	And Crocodile, opening his mouth even wider, answered,
Crocodile:	Ah-u!

Reader 6:	which must have meant "Of course."
Reader 1:	(Try yourself to say "of course" with your mouth open, only under no circumstances close it or else it won't work.)
Tari:	What a horror!
Reader 2:	Tari cried out after being in Crocodile's mouth about half a minute.
Tari:	It's simply frightful. All the things in this mouth. This is not a mouth, it's some kind of a . . .
Reader 3:	the little bird stammered, for she wanted to say, "swamp" but was afraid she'd offend Crocodile.
Tari:	You should see what all is in here!
Reader 4:	she continued.
Tari:	Even leeches. Black ones and the green ones and the ones with red stripes. It certainly is time you had your teeth cleaned.
Reader 5:	Hearing the mention of leeches, Crocodile sighed deeply.
Tari:	It's all right, it's all right. Soon everything will be shipshape.
Reader 6:	And Tari the bird went to work.
Reader 1:	Everybody was simply dumbstruck as they watched how Tari hopped from one of Crocodile's teeth to another, tapping with her beak in a knowing manner.
Reader 2:	Soon she joyfully announced:
Tari:	Here we are! Here's the hurting tooth! We'll pull it right out. It's going to hurt a little. One . . . two . . . three! All done!
Crocodile:	Ah-h,
Reader 3:	said Crocodile (meaning "ouch").

Reader 4:	And Tari sighed.
Tari:	Oh,
Reader 5:	she said, looking at the place where the tooth had been.
Tari:	Oh, there is another tooth growing right under it. How interesting!
Crocodile:	We always have that happen!
Reader 6:	Crocodile bragged,
Reader 1:	(by the way that's actually true)
Reader 2:	but since he never even for a second forgot that he wasn't supposed to close his mouth, what he said sounded like:
Reader 3:	**Ee-o-eh-eh.**
Reader 4:	So no one understood what he wanted to say.
Reader 5:	In five minutes everything was finished.
Reader 6:	The birds and the beasts could hardly believe it when the little bird Tari hopped out of the Crocodile's mouth all in one piece and completely unharmed.
Reader 1:	And you'd think that nothing more amazing could happen.
Reader 2:	But it did.
Reader 3:	When Crocodile finally closed his mouth, the first thing he said was:
Crocodile:	Thank you very, very much, you kind little bird! I feel much, much, much better!
Reader 4:	Hearing this, all the birds and beasts opened their own mouths so that Tari could clean their teeth as well.
Reader 5:	But that wouldn't work of course,
Reader 6:	(especially since birds don't have any kind of teeth, as you already know!)

Reader 1:	They were amazed because
Reader 2:	**A REAL TERRIBLE CROCODILE FOR THE FIRST TIME IN HIS LIFE ACTUALLY SAID A KIND WORD!**
Tari:	Think nothing of it,
Reader 3:	said Tari modestly to Crocodile.
Tari:	It's not worth thanking me for, considering that the leeches were of the best sort, especially those with the red stripes. If you'd like it, I'll clean your teeth every day!
Crocodile:	Would I like it!
Reader 4:	Crocodile exclaimed.
Tari:	All right. That's a deal,
Reader 5:	said Tari, and the monkeys suddenly clapped their hands,
Reader 6:	and all the other animals jumped and stomped with their hoofs,
Reader 1:	and the birds sang their happiest songs —
Reader 2:	though they didn't even know why.
Reader 3:	And so from that day on the little bird Tari has been called Ma-Tari-Kari,
Reader 4:	which in crocodile language means,
Reader 5:	a little bird which does big, kind deeds.
Reader 6:	and her nickname became **Crocodile's Toothbrush**.

A Readers Theatre Treasury of Stories

by Hazel Silliker
for 9 readers

Robot Doc

by Hazel Silliker

Reader 1:	Sal Franzo was a nice kid.
Reader 2:	People liked her.
Reader 3:	Robots liked her.
Reader 4:	But like everybody else, Sal had problems.
Reader 5:	Her family called her "Robot Doc,"
Reader 1:	and today her little hospital was jammed with sick robots.
Reader 2:	Sal glanced at the clock over her workbench. It read,
Reader 3:	Saturday, September 29, 2017, 08:42.
Sal:	Teki,
Reader 4:	called Sal.
Reader 5:	Teki was Sal's Tek-Tron robot.
Reader 1:	He was also her friend.
Reader 2:	Teki shuffled over to Sal.
Sal:	Teki, I've got problems.
Teki:	**OH NO. OH NO,**
Reader 3:	said Teki.
Sal:	Take it easy, pal. I'll live. But I could use some help.
Teki:	**SURE BOSS. SURE BOSS.**
Reader 4:	Sal laughed.
Sal:	Where did you get that "boss stuff?"
Reader 5:	Teki didn't answer, so Sal got to the point.
Sal:	Everybody is sick today,
Reader 1:	sighed Sal.

A Readers Theatre Treasury of Stories

Sal:	Mom wants me to fix Ultrastar. Uncle Angelo dropped off Empress II last night. And poor little Bolix has a broken arm.
Teki:	**OH NO. OH NO,**
Reader 2:	groaned Teki.
Sal:	Relax, I can fix Bolix. The problem is time. My time. Monday is science day at school. There's going to be a contest for the best nature collection. First prize is a solar bike.
Teki:	**OH NEAT. OH NEAT,**
Reader 3:	shouted Teki.
Sal:	Neat is right,
Reader 4:	agreed Sal.
Sal:	I really want to enter my rock collection. But I need more rocks. And I can't look for rocks and take care of all these patients at the same time.
Teki:	**ROCK ROCK ROCK. OKAY DOC!**
Reader 5:	Sal gave Teki a bear hug.
Sal:	**OUCH,**
Reader 1:	she cried. Teki was nice, but he was not soft.
Teki:	**ROCK FOR DOC. ROCK FOR DOC,**
Reader 2:	sang Teki as he shuffled out the door.
Reader 3:	Sal turned to Bolix with a smile.
Reader 4:	She felt better already.
Sal:	Okay, little guy,
Reader 5:	she said to the silent robot.
Sal:	Let's see if we can get that arm fixed up.
Reader 1:	Sal began by disconnecting Bolix's arm at the elbow.

Reader 2:	She saw at once that Bolix needed more than just body work.
Reader 3:	The arm circuit board had been damaged, too.
Sal:	Worse than I thought,
Reader 4:	mumbled Sal.

Reader 5:	Then a thought struck her.
Sal:	Where **did** Teki get that word — boss?
Reader 1:	she said out loud.
Sal:	I never programmed that in. I hope Teki's not coming down with something.

Reader 2:	Just then, Sal heard Teki on the stairs.
Teki:	**ROCK FOR DOC. ROCK FOR DOC**,
Reader 3:	sang Teki as he came through the door.
Reader 4:	He dropped a sock on the floor.
Sal:	Rock? That's a sock!
Teki:	**OH NO! OH NO!**
Sal:	Hey, it's okay. Don't worry.

Teki:	**ROCK FOR DOC. ROCK FOR DOC.**
Reader 5:	Teki turned and headed back out the door.
Reader 1:	Sal picked up the sock.
Reader 2:	She was puzzled.
Sal:	Take your time, Teki,
Reader 3:	she called.
Sal:	He's just trying too hard,
Reader 4:	thought Sal.

Sal:	Now where was I? Oh, yes, — Bolix,

Reader 5:	said Sal, returning to the little robot.
Sal:	What we have here is a tricky operation. Um...humm.

Reader 1:	Sal was interrupted by Teki.
Teki:	**ROCK FOR DOC. ROCK FOR DOC.**
Reader 2:	Teki shuffled in with a clock.
Reader 3:	Very gently, Sal said,
Sal:	Uh, that's a clock.
Reader 4:	Teki dropped the clock and headed for the door.
Reader 5:	He was moving fast.
Sal:	Hold it, Teki!
Reader 1:	shouted Sal.
Sal:	Maybe we should talk.
Reader 2:	But Teki didn't stop.
Reader 3:	Sal picked up the clock.
Reader 4:	It was a very old-fashioned clock, and she was surprised that Teki even knew it **was** a clock.

Sal:	**Smart robot**,
Reader 5:	she thought.
Sal:	But if he's so smart, Bolix, why isn't he finding rocks?
Reader 1:	Sal lifted Bolix's arm, but she was still thinking about Teki.

Sal:	**ROCK, SOCK, CLOCK,**
Reader 2:	she muttered.
Sal:	I see! Teki's finding rhymes! **GOOD GRIEF!** Teki must be sick, too!
Reader 3:	Bolix didn't say a word.

Sal:	What a day!
Reader 4:	groaned Sal.
Sal:	Robots all over the place, my rock collection needs work, and now Teki . . . too much!
Reader 5:	Sal put down Bolix's arm.
Reader 1:	She reached for her jacket.
Sal:	Enough is enough. If I can fix robots, I can fix my day! And step one is finding Teki.
Teki:	**ROCK FOR DOC. ROCK FOR DOC.**
Reader 2:	Sal put her hand over her eyes. What would Teki have this time?
Teki:	**ROCK FOR DOC. ROCK FOR DOC.**
Reader 3:	Teki came through the door wearing a flowered smock.
Sal:	Teki, my friend,
Reader 4:	said Sal with a smile,
Sal:	why don't we take the day off? We'll look over your circuits in the sunshine, have a picnic. . .
Reader 5:	Sal slung her arm over Teki's shoulder.
Teki:	**OKAY DOC. OKAY DOC.**
Reader 1:	And, Sal thought to herself,
Sal:	we'll keep our eyes open for rocks. . .